Birthday Letters

Birthday Letters   TED HUGHES

ff

faber and faber

First published in 1998
by Faber and Faber Limited
3 Queen Square London WC1N 3AU

This paperback edition first published in 1999

Photoset by Wilmaset Ltd, Birkenhead, Wirral
Printed in Italy

A CIP record for this book
is available from the British Library

ISBN 0-571-19473-7

10 9 8 7 6 5 4 3

for Frieda and Nicholas

Contents

Birthday Letters

Fulbright Scholars

Where was it, in the Strand? A display
Of news items, in photographs.
For some reason I noticed it.
A picture of that year's intake
Of Fulbright Scholars. Just arriving –
Or arrived. Or some of them.
Were you among them? I studied it,
Not too minutely, wondering
Which of them I might meet.
I remember that thought. Not
Your face. No doubt I scanned particularly
The girls. Maybe I noticed you.
Maybe I weighed you up, feeling unlikely.
Noted your long hair, loose waves –
Your Veronica Lake bang. Not what it hid.
It would appear blond. And your grin.
Your exaggerated American
Grin for the cameras, the judges, the strangers, the frighteners.
Then I forgot. Yet I remember
The picture: the Fulbright Scholars.
With their luggage? It seems unlikely.
Could they have come as a team? I was walking
Sore-footed, under hot sun, hot pavements.
Was it then I bought a peach? That's as I remember.
From a stall near Charing Cross Station.
It was the first fresh peach I had ever tasted.
I could hardly believe how delicious.
At twenty-five I was dumbfounded afresh
By my ignorance of the simplest things.

Caryatids (1)

What were those caryatids bearing?
It was the first poem of yours I had seen.
It was the only poem you ever wrote
That I disliked through the eyes of a stranger.
It seemed thin and brittle, the lines cold.
Like the theorem of a trap, a deadfall – set.
I saw that. And the trap unsprung, empty.
I felt no interest. No stirring
Of omen. In those days I coerced
Oracular assurance
In my favour out of every sign.
So missed everything
In the white, blindfolded, rigid faces
Of those women. I felt their frailty, yes:
Friable, burnt aluminium.
Fragile, like the mantle of a gas-lamp.
But made nothing
Of that massive, starless, mid-fall, falling
Heaven of granite
               stopped, as if in a snapshot,
By their hair.

Caryatids (2)

Stupid with confidence, in the playclothes
Of still growing, still reclining
In the cushioned palanquin,
The nursery care of nature's leisurely lift
Towards her fullness, we were careless
Of grave life, three of us, four, five, six –
Playing at friendship. Time in plenty
To test every role – for laughs,
For the experiment, lending our hours
To perversities of impulse, charade-like
Improvisations of the inane,
Like prisoners, our real life
Perforce deferred, with the real
World and self. So, playing at students, we filled
And drunkenly drained, filled and again drained
A boredom, a cornucopia
Of airy emptiness, of the brown
And the yellow ale, of makings and unmakings –
Godlike, as frivolous as faithless,
A dramaturgy of whim.
That was our education. The world
Crossed the wet courts, on Sunday, politely,
In tourists' tentative shoes.
All roads lay too open, opened too deeply
Every degree of the compass.
Here at the centre of the web, at the crossroads,
You published your poem
About Caryatids. We had heard
Of the dance of your blond veils, your flaring gestures,
Your misfit self-display. More to reach you
Than to reproach you, more to spark

A contact through the see-saw bustling
Atmospherics of higher learning
And lower socializing, than to correct you
With our archaic principles, we concocted
An attack, a dismemberment, laughing.
We had our own broadsheet to publish it.
Our Welshman composed it – still deaf
To the white noise of the elegy
That would fill his mouth and his ear
Worlds later, on Cader Idris,
In the wind and snow of your final climb.

Visit

Lucas, my friend, one
Among those three or four who stay unchanged
Like a separate self,
A stone in the bed of the river
Under every change, became your friend.
I heard of it, alerted. I was sitting
Youth away in an office near Slough,
Morning and evening between Slough and Holborn,
Hoarding wage to fund a leap to freedom
And the other side of the earth – a free-fall
To strip my chrysalis off me in the slipstream.
Weekends I recidived
Into Alma Mater. Girl-friend
Shared a supervisor and weekly session
With your American rival and you.
She detested you. She fed snapshots
Of you and she did not know what
Inflammable celluloid into my silent
Insatiable future, my blind-man's-buff
Internal torch of search. With my friend,
After midnight, I stood in a garden
Lobbing soil-clods up at a dark window.

Drunk, he was certain it was yours.
Half as drunk, I did not know he was wrong.
Nor did I know I was being auditioned
For the male lead in your drama,
Miming through the first easy movements
As if with eyes closed, feeling for the role.
As if a puppet were being tried on its strings,
Or a dead frog's legs touched by electrodes.

[7]

I jigged through those gestures – watched and judged
Only by starry darkness and a shadow.
Unknown to you and not knowing you.
Aiming to find you, and missing, and again missing.
Flinging earth at a glass that could not protect you
Because you were not there.

Ten years after your death
I meet on a page of your journal, as never before,
The shock of your joy
When you heard of that. Then the shock
Of your prayers. And under those prayers your panic
That prayers might not create the miracle,
Then, under the panic, the nightmare
That came rolling to crush you:
Your alternative – the unthinkable
Old despair and the new agony
Melting into one familiar hell.

Suddenly I read all this –
Your actual words, as they floated
Out through your throat and tongue and onto your page –
Just as when your daughter, years ago now,
Drifting in, gazing up into my face,
Mystified,
Where I worked alone
In the silent house, asked, suddenly:
'Daddy, where's Mummy?' The freezing soil
Of the garden, as I clawed it.
All round me that midnight's
Giant clock of frost. And somewhere
Inside it, wanting to feel nothing,
A pulse of fever. Somewhere

Inside that numbness of the earth
Our future trying to happen.
I look up – as if to meet your voice
With all its urgent future
That has burst in on me. Then look back
At the book of the printed words.
You are ten years dead. It is only a story.
Your story. My story.

Sam

It was all of a piece to you
That your horse, the white calm stallion, Sam,
Decided he'd had enough
And started home at a gallop. I can live
Your incredulity, your certainty
That this was it. You lost your stirrups. He galloped
Straight down the white line of the Barton Road.
You lost your reins, you lost your seat –
It was grab his neck and adore him
Or free-fall. You slewed under his neck,
An upside-down jockey with nothing
Between you and the cataract of macadam,
That horribly hard, swift river,
But the propeller terrors of his front legs
And the clangour of the iron shoes, so far beneath you.

Luck was already there. Did you have a helmet?
How did you cling on? Baby monkey
Using your arms and legs for clinging steel.
What saved you? Maybe your poems
Saved themselves, slung under that plunging neck,
Hammocked in your body over the switchback road.

You saw only blur. And a cyclist's shock-mask,
Fallen, dragging his bicycle over him, protective.
I can feel your bounced and dangling anguish,
Hugging what was left of your steerage.
How did you hang on? You couldn't have done it.
Something in you not you did it for itself.
You clung on, probably nearly unconscious,

Till he walked into his stable. That gallop
Was practice, but not enough, and quite useless.

When I jumped a fence you strangled me
One giddy moment, then fell off,
Flung yourself off and under my feet to trip me
And tripped me and lay dead. Over in a flash.

The Tender Place

Your temples, where the hair crowded in,
Were the tender place. Once to check
I dropped a file across the electrodes
Of a twelve-volt battery – it exploded
Like a grenade. Somebody wired you up.
Somebody pushed the lever. They crashed
The thunderbolt into your skull.
In their bleached coats, with blenched faces,
They hovered again
To see how you were, in your straps.
Whether your teeth were still whole.
The hand on the calibrated lever
Again feeling nothing
Except feeling nothing pushed to feel
Some squirm of sensation. Terror
Was the cloud of you
Waiting for these lightnings. I saw
An oak limb sheared at a bang.
You your Daddy's leg. How many seizures
Did you suffer this god to grab you
By the roots of the hair? The reports
Escaped back into clouds. What went up
Vaporized? Where lightning rods wept copper
And the nerve threw off its skin
Like a burning child
Scampering out of the bomb-flash. They dropped you
A rigid bent bit of wire
Across the Boston City grid. The lights
In the Senate House dipped
As your voice dived inwards

Right through the bolt-hole basement.
Came up, years later,
Over-exposed, like an X-ray –
Brain-map still dark-patched
With the scorched-earth scars
Of your retreat. And your words,
Faces reversed from the light,
Holding in their entrails.

St Botolph's

Our magazine was merely an overture
To the night and the party. I had predicted
Disastrous expense: a planetary
Certainty, according to Prospero's book.
Jupiter and the full moon conjunct
Opposed Venus. Disastrous expense
According to that book. Especially for me.
The conjunction combust my natal Sun.
Venus pinned exact on my mid-heaven.
For a wait-and-see astrologer – so what?
Touch of a bat's wing easily exorcised.
Our Chaucer would have stayed at home with his Dante.
Locating the planets more precisely,
He would have pondered it deeper. What else? I left it
For serious astrologers to worry
That conjunction, conjunct my Sun, conjunct
With your natal ruling Mars. And Chaucer
Would have pointed to that day's Sun in the Fish
Conjunct your Ascendant exactly
Opposite my Neptune and fixed
In my tenth House of good and evil fame.
Our Chaucer, I think, would have sighed.
He would have assured us, shaking his sorrowful head,
That day the solar system married us
Whether we knew it or not.

                              Falcon Yard:
Girl-friend like a loaded crossbow. The sound-waves
Jammed and torn by Joe Lyde's Jazz. The hall
Like the tilting deck of the *Titanic*:
A silent film, with that blare over it. Suddenly –
Lucas engineered it – suddenly you.

First sight. First snapshot isolated
Unalterable, stilled in the camera's glare.
Taller
Than ever you were again. Swaying so slender
It seemed your long, perfect, American legs
Simply went on up. That flaring hand,
Those long, balletic, monkey-elegant fingers.
And the face – a tight ball of joy.
I see you there, clearer, more real
Than in any of the years in its shadow –
As if I saw you that once, then never again.
The loose fall of hair – that floppy curtain
Over your face, over your scar. And your face
A rubbery ball of joy
Round the African-lipped, laughing, thickly
Crimson-painted mouth. And your eyes
Squeezed in your face, a crush of diamonds,
Incredibly bright, bright as a crush of tears
That might have been tears of joy, a squeeze of joy.
You meant to knock me out
With your vivacity. I remember
Little from the rest of that evening.
I slid away with my girl-friend. Nothing
Except her hissing rage in a doorway
And my stupefied interrogation
Of your blue headscarf from my pocket
And the swelling ring-moat of tooth-marks
That was to brand my face for the next month.
The me beneath it for good.

The Shot

Your worship needed a god.
Where it lacked one, it found one.
Ordinary jocks became gods –
Deified by your infatuation
That seemed to have been designed at birth for a god.
It was a god-seeker. A god-finder.
Your Daddy had been aiming you at God
When his death touched the trigger.

                                        In that flash
You saw your whole life. You ricocheted
The length of your Alpha career
With the fury
Of a high-velocity bullet
That cannot shed one foot-pound
Of kinetic energy. The elect
More or less died on impact –
They were too mortal to take it. They were mind-stuff,
Provisional, speculative, mere auras.
Sound-barrier events along your flightpath.
But inside your sob-sodden Kleenex
And your Saturday night panics,
Under your hair done this way and done that way,
Behind what looked like rebounds
And the cascade of cries diminuendo,
You were undeflected.
You were gold-jacketed, solid silver,
Nickel-tipped. Trajectory perfect
As through ether. Even the cheek-scar,
Where you seemed to have side-swiped concrete,
Served as a rifling groove

To keep you true.
                    Till your real target
Hid behind me. Your Daddy,
The god with the smoking gun. For a long time
Vague as mist, I did not even know
I had been hit,
Or that you had gone clean through me –
To bury yourself at last in the heart of the god.

In my position, the right witchdoctor
Might have caught you in flight with his bare hands,
Tossed you, cooling, one hand to the other,
Godless, happy, quieted.
                    I managed
A wisp of your hair, your ring, your watch, your nightgown.

Trophies

The panther? It had already dragged you
As if in its jaws, across Europe.
As if trailing between its legs,
Your mouth crying open, or not even crying any more,
Just letting yourself be dragged. Its real prey
Had skipped and escaped. So the fangs,
Blind in frustration,
Crushed your trachea, strangled the sounds. The Rorschach
Splashing of those outpourings stained
Your journal pages. Your effort to cry words
Came apart in aired blood
Enriched by the adrenalins
Of despair, terror, sheer fury –
After forty years
The whiff of that beast, off the dry pages,
Lifts the hair on the back of my hands.
The thrill of it. The sudden
Look that locked on me
Through your amber jewels
And as I caught you lolling locked
Its jaws into my face. The tenacity
Of the big cat's claim
On the one marked down and once disabled
Is a chemical process – a combustion
Of the stuff of judgement.

So it sprang over you. Its jungle prints
Hit your page. Plainly the blood
Was your own. With a laugh I
Took its full weight. Little did I know
The shock attack of a big predator

According to survivors numbs the target
Into drunken euphoria. Still smiling
As it carried me off I detached
The hairband carefully from between its teeth
And a ring from its ear, for my trophies.

18 Rugby Street

So there in Number Eighteen Rugby Street's
Victorian torpor and squalor I waited for you.
I think of that house as a stage-set –
Four floors exposed to the auditorium.
On all four floors, in, out, the love-struggle
In all its acts and scenes, a snakes and ladders
Of intertangling and of disentangling
Limbs and loves and lives. Nobody was old.
An unmysterious laboratory of amours.
Perpetual performance – names of the actors altered,
But never the parts. They told me: 'You
Should write a book about this house. It's possessed!
Whoever comes into it never gets properly out!
Whoever enters it enters a labyrinth –
A Knossos of coincidence! And now you're in it.'
The legends were amazing. I listened, amazed.

I lived there alone. Sat alone
At the hacked, archaic, joiner's bench
That did for desk and table,
And waited for you and Lucas.
Whatever I was thinking I was not thinking
Of that Belgian girl in the ground-floor flat,
Plump as a mushroom, hair black as boot polish:
The caged bird and extra-marital cuddle
Of the second-hand-car dealer who kept
The catacomb basement heaped with exhaust mufflers,
Assorted jagged shards of cars, shin-rippers
On the way to the unlit and unlovely
Lavatory beneath the street's pavement.
That girl had nothing to do with the rest of the house

But play her part in the drama. Her house-jailor
Who kept her in solitary was a demon
High-explosive, black, insane Alsatian
That challenged through the chained crack of the door
Every entrance and exit. He guarded her,
For the car dealer, from all, too well finally.
Not, seven years in the future, from her gas-oven.
She was nothing to do with me. Nor was Susan
Who still had to be caught in the labyrinth,
And who would meet the Minotaur there,
And would be holding me from my telephone
Those nights you would most need me. On this evening
Nothing could make me think I would ever be needed
By anybody. Ten years had to darken,
Three of them in your grave, before Susan
Could pace that floor above night after night
(Where you and I, the new rings big on our fingers,
Had warmed our wedding night in the single bed)
Crying alone and dying of leukaemia.

Lucas was bringing you. You were pausing
A night in London on your escape to Paris.
April 13th, your father's birthday. A Friday.
I guessed you were off to whirl through some euphoric
American Europe. Years after your death
I learned the desperation of that search
Through those following days, scattering your tears
Around the cobbles of Paris. I deferred for a night
Your panics, your fevers, your worst fear –
The toad-stone in the head of your desolation.
The dream you hunted for, the life you begged
To be given again, you would never recover, ever.
Your journal told me the story of your torture.

I guess how you visited each of your sacred shrines
In raging faith you'd catch him there, somehow,
By clairvoyance, by coincidence –
Normally child's play to a serious passion.
This was not the last time it would fail you.
Meanwhile there was me, for a few hours –
A few pence on the fare, for insurance.
Happy to be martyred for folly
I invoked you, bribing Fate to produce you.
Were you conjuring me? I had no idea
How I was becoming necessary,
Or what emergency surgery Fate would make
Of my casual self-service. I can hear you
Climbing the bare stairs, alive and close,
Babbling to be overheard, breathless.
That was your artillery, to confuse me:
Before coming over the top in your panoply
You wanted me to hear you panting. Then –
Blank. How did you enter? What came next?
How did Lucas delete himself, for instance?
Did we even sit? A great bird, you
Surged in the plumage of your excitement,
Raving exhilaration. A blueish voltage –
Fluorescent cobalt, a flare of aura
That I later learned was yours uniquely.
And your eyes' peculiar brightness, their oddness,
Two little brown people, hooded, Prussian,
But elvish, and girlish, and sparking
With the pressure of your effervescence.
Were they family heirlooms, as in your son?
For me yours were the novel originals.
And now at last I got a good look at you.
Your roundy face, that your friends, being objective,

Called 'rubbery' and you, crueller, 'boneless':
A device for elastic extremes,
A spirit mask transfigured every moment
In its own séance, its own ether.
And I became aware of the mystery
Of your lips, like nothing before in my life,
Their aboriginal thickness. And of your nose,
Broad and Apache, nearly a boxer's nose,
Scorpio's obverse to the Semitic eagle
That made every camera your enemy,
The jailor of your vanity, the traitor
In your Sexual Dreams Incorporated,
Nose from Attila's horde: a prototype face
That could have looked up at me through the smoke
Of a Navajo campfire. And your small temples
Into which your hair-roots crowded, upstaged
By that glamorous, fashionable bang.
And your little chin, your Pisces chin.
It was never a face in itself. Never the same.
It was like the sea's face – a stage
For weathers and currents, the sun's play and the moon's.
Never a face until that final morning
When it became the face of a child – its scar
Like a Maker's flaw. But now you declaimed
A long poem about a black panther
While I held you and kissed you and tried to keep you
From flying about the room. For all that,
You would not stay.

We walked south across London to Fetter Lane
And your hotel. Opposite the entrance
On a bombsite becoming a building site
We clutched each other giddily

For safety and went in a barrel together
Over some Niagara. Falling
In the roar of soul your scar told me –
Like its secret name or its password –
How you had tried to kill yourself. And I heard
Without ceasing for a moment to kiss you
As if a sober star had whispered it
Above the revolving, rumbling city: stay clear.

A poltroon of a star. I cannot remember
How I smuggled myself, wrapped in you,
Into the hotel. There we were.
You were slim and lithe and smooth as a fish.
You were a new world. My new world.
So this is America, I marvelled.
Beautiful, beautiful America!

The Machine

The dark ate at you. And the fear
Of being crushed. 'A huge dark machine',
'The grinding indifferent
Millstone of circumstance'. After
Watching the orange sunset, these were the words
You put on a page. They had come to you
When I did not. When you tried
To will me up the stair, this terror
Arrived instead. While I
Most likely was just sitting,
Maybe with Lucas, no more purpose in me
Than in my own dog
That I did not have. A real dog
Might have stared at nothing
Hair on end
While the grotesque mask of your Mummy-Daddy
Half-quarry, half-hospital, whole
Juggernaut, stuffed with your unwritten poems,
Ground invisibly without a ripple
Towards me through the unstirred willows,
Through the wall of The Anchor,
Drained my Guinness at a gulp,
Blackly yawned me
Into its otherworld interior
Where I would find my home. My children. And my life
Forever trying to climb the steps now stone
Towards the door now red
Which you, in your own likeness, would open
With still time to talk.

God Help the Wolf after Whom the Dogs Do Not Bark

There you met it – the mystery of hatred.
After your billions of years in anonymous matter
That was where you were found – and promptly hated.
You tried your utmost to reach and touch those people
With gifts of yourself –
Just like your first words as a toddler
When you rushed at every visitor to the house
Clasping their legs and crying: 'I love you! I love you!'
Just as you had danced for your father
In the home of anger – gifts of your life
To sweeten his slow death and mix yourself in it
Where he lay propped on the couch,
To sugar the bitterness of his raging death.

You searched for yourself to go on giving it
As if after the nightfall of his going
You danced on in the dark house,
Eight years old, in your tinsel.

Searching for yourself, in the dark, as you danced,
Floundering a little, crying softly,
Like somebody searching for somebody drowning
In dark water,
Listening for them – in panic at losing
Those listening seconds from your searching –
Then dancing wilder in the silence.

The Colleges lifted their heads. It did seem
You disturbed something just perfected
That they were holding carefully, all of a piece,
Till the glue dried. And as if

Reporting some felony to the police
They let you know that you were not John Donne.
You no longer care. Did you save their names?
But then they let you know, day by day,
Their contempt for everything you attempted,
Took pains to inject their bile, as for your health,
Into your morning coffee. Even signed
Their homeopathic letters,
Envelopes full of carefully broken glass
To lodge behind your eyes so you would see

Nobody wanted your dance,
Nobody wanted your strange glitter – your floundering
Drowning life and your effort to save yourself,
Treading water, dancing the dark turmoil,
Looking for something to give –
                              Whatever you found
They bombarded with splinters,
Derision, mud – the mystery of that hatred.

Fidelity

It was somewhere to live. I was
Just hanging around, courting you,
Afloat on the morning tide and tipsy feelings
Of my twenty-fifth year. Gutted, restyled
À la mode, the Alexandra House
Became a soup-kitchen. Those were the days
Before the avant-garde of coffee bars.
The canteen clatter of the British Restaurant,
One of the war's utility leftovers,
Was still the place to repair the nights with breakfasts.
But Alexandra House was the place to be seen in.
The girls that helped to run it lived above it
With a retinue of loose-lifers, day-sleepers
Exhausted with night-owling. Somehow
I got a mattress up there, in a top room,
Overlooking Petty Cury. A bare
Mattress, on bare boards, in a bare room.
All I had, my notebook and that mattress.
Under the opening, bud-sticky chestnuts,
On into June, my job chucked, I laboured
Only at you, squandering all I'd saved.
Free of University I dangled
In its liberties. Every night
I slept on that mattress, under one blanket,
With a lovely girl, escaped freshly
From her husband to the frontier exposure
Of work in the soup-kitchen. What
Knighthood possessed me there? I think of it
As a kind of time that cannot pass,
That I never used, so still possess.

She and I slept in each other's arms,
Naked and easy as lovers, a month of nights,
Yet never once made love. A holy law
Had invented itself, somehow, for me.
But she too served it, like a priestess,
Tender, kind and stark naked beside me.
She traced out the fresh rips you had inscribed
Across my back, seeming to join me
In my obsession, in my concentration,
To keep my preoccupation intact.
She never once invited, never tempted.
And I never stirred a finger beyond
Sisterly comforting. I was like her sister.
It never seemed unnatural. I was focused,
So locked onto you, so brilliantly,
Everything that was not you was blind-spot.
I still puzzle over it – doubtful, now,
Whether to envy myself, or pity. Her friend,
Who had a bigger room, was wilder.
We moved in with her. That lofty room
Became a dormitory and HQ
Alternative to St Botolph's. Plump and pretty,
With a shameless gap-tooth laugh, her friend
Did all she could to get me inside her.
And you will never know what a battle
I fought to keep the meaning of my words
Solid with the world we were making.
I was afraid, if I lost that fight
Something might abandon us. Lifting
Each of those naked girls, as they smiled at me
In their early twenties, I laid them
Under the threshold of our unlikely future

As those who wanted protection for a new home
Used to bury, under the new threshold,
A sinless child.

Fate Playing

Because the message somehow met a goblin,
Because precedents tripped your expectations,
Because your London was still a kaleidoscope
Of names and places any jolt could scramble,
You waited mistaken. The bus from the North
Came in and emptied and I was not on it.
No matter how much you insisted
And begged the driver, probably with tears,
To produce me or to remember seeing me
Just miss getting on. I was not on it.
Eight in the evening and I was lost and at large
Somewhere in England. You restrained
Your confident inspiration
And did not dash out into the traffic
Milling around Victoria, utterly certain
Of bumping into me where I would have to be walking.
I was not walking anywhere. I was sitting
Unperturbed, in my seat on the train
Rocking towards King's Cross. Somebody,
Calmer than you, had a suggestion. So,
When I got off the train, expecting to find you
Somewhere down at the root of the platform,
I saw that surge and agitation, a figure
Breasting the flow of released passengers,
Then your molten face, your molten eyes
And your exclamations, your flinging arms
Your scattering tears
As if I had come back from the dead
Against every possibility, against
Every negative but your own prayer
To your own gods. There I knew what it was

To be a miracle. And behind you
Your jolly taxi-driver, laughing, like a small god,
To see an American girl being so American,
And to see your frenzied chariot-ride –
Sobbing and goading him, and pleading with him
To make happen what you needed to happen –
Succeed so completely, thanks to him.
Well, it was a wonder
That my train was not earlier, even much earlier,
That it pulled in, late, the very moment
You irrupted onto the platform. It was
Natural and miraculous and an omen
Confirming everything
You wanted confirmed. So your huge despair,
Your cross-London panic dash
And now your triumph, splashed over me,
Like love forty-nine times magnified,
Like the first thunder cloudburst engulfing
The drought in August
When the whole cracked earth seems to quake
And every leaf trembles
And everything holds up its arms weeping.

The Owl

I saw my world again through your eyes
As I would see it again through your children's eyes.
Through your eyes it was foreign.
Plain hedge hawthorns were peculiar aliens,
A mystery of peculiar lore and doings.
Anything wild, on legs, in your eyes
Emerged at a point of exclamation
As if it had appeared to dinner guests
In the middle of the table. Common mallards
Were artefacts of some unearthliness,
Their wooings were a hypnagogic film
Unreeled by the river. Impossible
To comprehend the comfort of their feet
In the freezing water. You were a camera
Recording reflections you could not fathom.
I made my world perform its utmost for you.
You took it all in with an incredulous joy
Like a mother handed her new baby
By the midwife. Your frenzy made me giddy.
It woke up my dumb, ecstatic boyhood
Of fifteen years before. My masterpiece
Came that black night on the Grantchester road.
I sucked the throaty thin woe of a rabbit
Out of my wetted knuckle, by a copse
Where a tawny owl was enquiring.
Suddenly it swooped up, splaying its pinions
Into my face, taking me for a post.

A Pink Wool Knitted Dress

In your pink wool knitted dress
Before anything had smudged anything
You stood at the altar. Bloomsday.

Rain – so that a just-bought umbrella
Was the only furnishing about me
Newer than three years inured.
My tie – sole, drab, veteran RAF black –
Was the used-up symbol of a tie.
My cord jacket – thrice-dyed black, exhausted,
Just hanging on to itself.

I was a post-war, utility son-in-law!
Not quite the Frog-Prince. Maybe the Swineherd
Stealing this daughter's pedigree dreams
From under her watchtowered searchlit future.

No ceremony could conscript me
Out of my uniform. I wore my whole wardrobe –
Except for the odd, spare, identical item.
My wedding, like Nature, wanted to hide.
However – if we were going to be married
It had better be Westminster Abbey. Why not?
The Dean told us why not. That is how
I learned that I had a Parish Church.
St George of the Chimney Sweeps.
So we squeezed into marriage finally.
Your mother, brave even in this
US Foreign Affairs gamble,
Acted all bridesmaids and all guests,
Even – magnanimity – represented

My family
Who had heard nothing about it.
I had invited only their ancestors.
I had not even confided my theft of you
To a closest friend. For Best Man – my squire
To hold the meanwhile rings –
We requisitioned the sexton. Twist of the outrage:
He was packing children into a bus,
Taking them to the Zoo – in that downpour!
All the prison animals had to be patient
While we married.
                              You were transfigured.
So slender and new and naked,
A nodding spray of wet lilac.
You shook, you sobbed with joy, you were ocean depth
Brimming with God.
You said you saw the heavens open
And show riches, ready to drop upon us.
Levitated beside you, I stood subjected
To a strange tense: the spellbound future.

In that echo-gaunt, weekday chancel
I see you
Wrestling to contain your flames
In your pink wool knitted dress
And in your eye-pupils – great cut jewels
Jostling their tear-flames, truly like big jewels
Shaken in a dice-cup and held up to me.

Your Paris

Your Paris, I thought, was American.
I wanted to humour you.
When you stepped, in a shatter of exclamations,
Out of the Hôtel des Deux Continents
Through frame after frame,
Street after street, of Impressionist paintings,
Under the chestnut shades of Hemingway,
Fitzgerald, Henry Miller, Gertrude Stein,
I kept my Paris from you. My Paris
Was only just not German. The capital
Of the Occupation and old nightmare.
I read each bullet scar in the Quai stonework
With an eerie familiar feeling,
And stared at the stricken, sunny exposure of pavement
Beneath it. I had rehearsed
Carefully, over and over, just those moments –
Most of my life, it seemed. While you
Called me Aristide Bruant and wanted
To draw *les toits*, and your ecstasies ricocheted
Off the walls patched and scabbed with posters –
I heard the contrabasso counterpoint
In my dog-nosed pondering analysis
Of café chairs where the SS mannequins
Had performed their *tableaux vivants*
So recently the coffee was still bitter
As acorns, and the waiters' eyes
Clogged with dregs of betrayal, reprisal, hatred.
I was not much ravished by the view of the roofs.
My Paris was a post-war utility survivor,
The stink of fear still hanging in the wardrobes,
Collaborateurs barely out of their twenties,

Every other face closed by the Camps
Or the Maquis. I was a ghostwatcher.
My perspectives were veiled by what rose
Like methane from the reopened
Mass grave of Verdun. For you all that
Was the anecdotal aesthetic touch
On Picasso's portrait
Of Apollinaire, with its proleptic
Marker for the bullet. And wherever
Your eye lit, your immaculate palette,
The thesaurus of your cries,
Touched in its tints and textures. Your lingo
Always like an emergency burn-off
To protect you from spontaneous combustion
Protected you
And your Paris. It was diesel aflame
To the dog in me. It scorched up
Every scent and sensor. And it sealed
The underground, your hide-out,
That chamber, where you still hung waiting
For your torturer
To remember his amusement. Those walls,
Raggy with posters, were your own flayed skin –
Stretched on your stone god.
What walked beside me was flayed,
One walking wound that the air
Coming against kept in a fever, wincing
To agonies. Your practised lips
Translated the spasms to what you excused
As your gushy burblings – which I decoded
Into a language, utterly new to me
With conjectural, hopelessly wrong meanings –
You gave me no hint how, at every corner,

[37]

My fingers linked in yours, you expected
The final face-to-face revelation
To grab your whole body. Your Paris
Was a desk in a *pension*
Where your letters
Waited for him unopened. Was a labyrinth
Where you still hurtled, scattering tears.
Was a dream where you could not
Wake or find the exit or
The Minotaur to put a blessed end
To the torment. What searching miles
Did you drag your pain
That were for me plain paving, albeit
Pecked by the odd, stray, historic bullet.
The mere dog in me, happy to protect you
From your agitation and your stone hours,
Like a guide dog, loyal to correct your stumblings,
Yawned and dozed and watched you calm yourself
With your anaesthetic – your drawing, as by touch,
Roofs, a traffic bollard, a bottle, me.

You Hated Spain

                    Spain frightened you. Spain
Where I felt at home. The blood-raw light,
The oiled anchovy faces, the African
Black edges to everything, frightened you.
Your schooling had somehow neglected Spain.
The wrought-iron grille, death and the Arab drum.
You did not know the language, your soul was empty
Of the signs, and the welding light
Made your blood shrivel. Bosch
Held out a spidery hand and you took it
Timidly, a bobby-sox American.
You saw right down to the Goya funeral grin
And recognized it, and recoiled
As your poems winced into chill, as your panic
Clutched back towards college America.
So we sat as tourists at the bullfight
Watching bewildered bulls awkwardly butchered,
Seeing the grey-faced matador, at the barrier
Just below us, straightening his bent sword
And vomiting with fear. And the horn
That hid itself inside the blowfly belly
Of the toppled picador punctured
What was waiting for you. Spain
Was the land of your dreams: the dust-red cadaver
You dared not wake with, the puckering amputations
No literature course had glamorized.
The juju land behind your African lips.
Spain was what you tried to wake up from
And could not. I see you, in moonlight,
Walking the empty wharf at Alicante
Like a soul waiting for the ferry,

A new soul, still not understanding,
Thinking it is still your honeymoon
In the happy world, with your whole life waiting,
Happy, and all your poems still to be found.

Moonwalk

A glare chunk of moon.
The hill no colour
Under the polarized light.
Like a day pushed inside out. Everything
In negative. Your mask
Bleak as cut iron, a shell-half –
Shucked off the moon. Alarming
And angering moon-devil – here somewhere.
The Ancient Mariner's Death-in-Life woman
Straight off the sea's fevered incandescence
Throwing black-and-white dice.
A sea saracen and cruel-looking.
And your words
Like bits of beetles and spiders
Retched out by owls. Fluorescent,
Blue-black, splintered. Bat-skulls. One day, I thought,
I shall understand this tomb-Egyptian,
This talking in tongues to a moon-mushroom.
Never wake a sleepwalker. Let the blame
Hit the olive-trees.
The black blood of their shadows
Might cry out like Abel's.
Who's here? That's the question: Who's here?
The doctor who humours, and watches
As the patient dies in his care.
Something else shares the skin of the day.
The mimicry of possession, the set of the mouth,
Would be awful in a dream. Awake
It's a question of patience. Like a phantom
Womb-tumour. The full moon of radium
Had stripped herself for the operation –

Stripped herself of everything
But moon. What is moon? The raw lump
Of ore, not yet smelted and shaped
Into your managed talent. Or it flings
Onto the X-ray plate the shape of the ape
Being led by the virgin, both helpless
In her hell. The moon
Takes things like that seriously –
As it stares at the kitchen implements.

I was the gnat in the ear of the wounded
Elephant of my own
Incomprehension. Curator
Of the tar-pit. Around us
On the moon-brown hills, the stars rested
Their possible anaesthesia,
All the mythologies, all inaccessible.
The sardine-boats – off with Cassiopeia.
Every stone a rosetta
Of moon-marks. I could no more join you
Than on the sacrificial slab
That you were looking for. I could not
Even imagine the priest. I walked beside you
As if seeing you for the first time –
The moon-shadow of a strange dog,
The silent shadow of a dog
That had befriended you. Your eyes
Were in their element
But uncomprehending and
Terrified by it. Like the surfaced Kraken
You took in the round
Of moon and starred sea, littered heaven and
Moon-blanched, moon-trenched sea-town

[42]

And its hook of promontory halving
The two wings of beach. A great bird
Fallen beside the Mediterranean.
A sea of lapis lazuli painted
Glitteringly afresh, just for you,
By de Chirico.
You carried it all, like shards and moults on a tray,
To be reassembled
In the poem to be written so prettily,
And to be worn like a fiesta mask
By the daemon that gazed through it
As through empty sockets – that still gazes
Through it at me.

Drawing

Drawing calmed you. Your poker infernal pen
Was like a branding iron. Objects
Suffered into their new presence, tortured
Into final position. As you drew
I felt released, calm. Time opened
When you drew the market at Benidorm.
I sat near you, scribbling something.
Hours burned away. The stall-keepers
Kept coming to see you had them properly.
We sat on those steps, in our rope-soles,
And were happy. Our tourist novelty
Had worn off, we knew our own ways
Through the town's runs. We were familiar
Foreign objects. When he'd sold his bananas
The banana seller gave us a solo
Violin performance on his banana stalk.
Everybody crowded to praise your drawing.
You drew doggedly on, arresting details,
Till you had the whole scene imprisoned.
Here it is. You rescued for ever
Our otherwise lost morning. Your patience,
Your lip-gnawing scowl, got the portrait
Of a market-place that still slept
In the Middle Ages. Just before
It woke and disappeared
Under the screams of a million summer migrants
And the cliff of dazzling hotels. As your hand
Went under Heptonstall to be held
By endless darkness. While my pen travels on
Only two hundred miles from your hand,
Holding this memory of your red, white-spotted bandanna,

Your shorts, your short-sleeved jumper –
One of the thirty I lugged around Europe –
And your long brown legs, propping your pad,
And the contemplative calm
I drank from your concentrated quiet,
In this contemplative calm
Now I drink from your stillness that neither
Of us can disturb or escape.

Fever

You had a fever. You had a real ailment.
You had eaten a baddie.
You lay helpless and a little bit crazy
With the fever. You cried for America
And its medicine cupboard. You tossed
On the immovable Spanish galleon of a bed
In the shuttered Spanish house
That the sunstruck outside glare peered into
As into a tomb. 'Help me,' you whispered, 'help me.'

You rambled. You dreamed you were clambering
Into the well-hatch and, waking, you wanted
To clamber into the well-hatch – the all-clear
Short cut to the cool of the water,
The cool of the dark shaft, the best place
To find oblivion from your burning tangle
And the foreign bug. You cried for certain
You were going to die.
                              I bustled about.
I was nursemaid. I fancied myself at that.
I liked the crisis of the vital role.
I felt things had become real. Suddenly mother,
As a familiar voice, woke in me.
She arrived with the certain knowledge. I made a huge soup.
Carrots, tomatoes, peppers and onions,
A rainbow stir of steaming elixir. You
Had to become a sluice, a conduit
Of pure vitamin C. I promised you,
This had saved Voltaire from the plague.
I had to saturate you and flush you

With this simmer of essences.
                                    I spooned it
Into your helpless, baby-bird gape, gently,
Masterfully, patiently, hour by hour.
I wiped your tear-ruined face, your exhausted face,
All loose with woe and abandon.
I spooned more and you gulped it like life,
Sobbing 'I'm going to die.'
                                    As I paused
Between your mouthfuls, I stared at the readings
On your dials. Your cry jammed so hard
Over into the red of catastrophe
Left no space for worse. And I thought
How sick is she? Is she exaggerating?
And I recoiled, just a little,
Just for balance, just for symmetry,
Into sceptical patience, a little.
If it can be borne, why make so much of it?
'Come on, now,' I soothed. 'Don't be so scared.
It's only a bug, don't let it run away with you.'

What I was really saying was: 'Stop crying wolf.'
Other thoughts, chilly, familiar thoughts,
Came across the tightrope: 'Stop crying wolf,
Or else I shall not know, I shall not hear
When things get really bad.'
                                    It seemed easy
Watching such thoughts come up in such good time.
Plenty of time to think: 'She is crying
As if the most impossible of all
Horrible things had happened –
Had already happened, was going on
Still happening, with the whole world

Too late to help.' Then the blank thought
Of the anaesthesia that helps creatures
Under the polar ice, and the callous
That eases overwhelmed doctors. A twisting thought
Of the overload of dilemma, the white-out,
That brings baffled planarian worms to a standstill
Where they curl up and die.

You were overloaded. I said nothing.
I said nothing. The stone man made soup.
The burning woman drank it.

55 Eltisley

Our first home has forgotten us.
I saw when I drove past it
How slight our lives had been
To have left not a trace. When we first moved in there
I looked for omens.
Vacated by a widow gathered to her family
All it told me was: 'Her life is over.'
She had left the last blood of her husband
Staining a pillow. Their whole story
Hung – a miasma – round that stain.
Senility's sour odour. It had condensed
Like a grease on the cutlery. It confirmed
Your idea of England: part
Nursing home, part morgue
For something partly dying, partly dead.
Just so the grease-grimed shelves, the tacky, dark walls
Of the hutch of a kitchen revolted you
Into a fury of scouring. I studied the blood.
Was it mouth-blood, or ear-blood,
Or the blood of a head-wound, after some fall?
I took possession before
Anything of ours had reconditioned
That crypt of old griefs and its stale gas
Of a dead husband. I claimed our first home
Alone and slept in it alone,
Only trying not to inhale the ghost
That clung on in the breath of the bed.
His death and her bereavement
Were the sole guests at our house-warming.
We splurged ten pounds on a sumptuous Chesterfield
Of Prussian blue velvet. Our emergency

[49]

Kit of kitchen gadgets adapted
That rented, abandoned, used-up grubbiness
To the shipyard and ritual launching
Of our expedition. One mirage
Of the world as it is and has to be
Seemed no worse than another. Already
We were beyond the Albatross.
You yourself were a whole Antarctic sea
Between me and your girl-friends. You were pack-ice
Between me and any possible mention
Of my might-have-beens. I had accepted
The meteorological phenomena
That kept your compass steady.
Like polar apparitions only Wendy
And Dorothea, by being visionary
Fairy godmothers, were forgiven their faces.
I pitied your delirium of suspicion.
Through the rainbow darkness I plodded,
Following a clue of Patanjali.
Hand in hand we plodded. For me, that home
Was our first camp, our first winter,
Where I was happy to stare at a candle.
For you, it was igloo comfort.
Your Bell Jar centrally heated
By a stupefying paraffin heater.
But you were happy too, warming your hands
At the crystal ball
Of your heirloom paperweight. Inside it,
There, in miniature, was your New England Christmas,
A Mummy and a Daddy, still together
Under the whirling snow, and our future.

Chaucer

'Whan that Aprille with his shoures soote
The droghte of March hath perced to the roote . . .'
At the top of your voice, where you swayed on the top of a stile,
Your arms raised – somewhat for balance, somewhat
To hold the reins of the straining attention
Of your imagined audience – you declaimed Chaucer
To a field of cows. And the Spring sky had done it
With its flying laundry, and the new emerald
Of the thorns, the hawthorn, the blackthorn,
And one of those bumpers of champagne
You snatched unpredictably from pure spirit.
Your voice went over the fields towards Grantchester.
It must have sounded lost. But the cows
Watched, then approached: they appreciated Chaucer.
You went on and on. Here were reasons
To recite Chaucer. Then came the Wyf of Bath,
Your favourite character in all literature.
You were rapt. And the cows were enthralled.
They shoved and jostled shoulders, making a ring,
To gaze into your face, with occasional snorts
Of exclamation, renewed their astounded attention,
Ears angling to catch every inflection,
Keeping their awed six feet of reverence
Away from you. You just could not believe it.
And you could not stop. What would happen
If you were to stop? Would they attack you,
Scared by the shock of silence, or wanting more – ?
So you had to go on. You went on –
And twenty cows stayed with you hypnotized.
How did you stop? I can't remember
You stopping. I imagine they reeled away –

[51]

Rolling eyes, as if driven from their fodder.
I imagine I shooed them away. But
Your sostenuto rendering of Chaucer
Was already perpetual. What followed
Found my attention too full
And had to go back into oblivion.

Ouija

Always bad news from the Ouija board.
We spelt out the alphabet, fringed the arena
Of your coffee table with the letters.
Two goals: 'Yes' at one end, 'No' at the other.
Then leaned, our middle fingers lolling
On the bottom of the upturned glass. Frivolity
Darkening to solemn apprehension.
Respectfully, we summoned a spirit.
It was easy as fishing for eels
In the warm summer darkness. Hardly a minute
Before the glass began to nose at the letters,
Then to circle thoughtfully. Finally, 'Yes'.
Something was there. A spirit offered to be named.
She nudged out her name. And she was
Despairing, depressed, pathetic. She concocted
Macabre, gloomy answers. Every answer
Was 'rottenness' or 'worms' or simply 'bones'.
She left a peculiar guilt – a befouled
Feeling of jeopardy, a sense that days
Would be needed now to cleanse us
Of the pollution. Some occult pickpocket
Had slit the soul's silk and fingered us.
But we explained it easily: some rejected
Dream's drop-out had found its way to the glass
Where the power had gone to its head.

                                        Far better

We fish up discredited clairvoyance,
Assume we hummed on all creation's wavelengths,
Attune Ouija to the frequencies
Of omniscience, of prophecy.
A case of locating the right spirit.

[53]

Once again we leaned
Over the brink of letters and called down
Into the well of Ouija. This time
We announced the requirements in firm tones,
And as the glass began to prowl repeated
Clearly the qualifications for the job.
Suddenly the glass, with a whizzing flourish,
Was wrenched almost from under our fingers to 'Yes'.
As if we'd hooked a fish right there at the surface.
This one promised only truth. To prove it
He offered to fill in that week's football coupon
And make our fortune in the next five minutes.
He picked thirteen draws. 'That's not many.'
'Just enough,' he replied. He was right –
But spaced all down the column of matches
His accurately picked-off thirteen draws,
The whole clutch, were adrift by a single match
Ahead of the day's results. 'Too eager?' 'Yes.'
He apologized. He swore to correct himself.
Five days then of tiptoe internal hush.
Finally the stalk, the taking aim –
And there again he got the total number,
Eighteen, precisely. But his cluster, spot on
If it had not been split
And adrift in two groups in opposite directions –
Two before, three behind – fell
Through the safety nets I'd spread for his errors.
'Gambling fever's beginning to give him the shakes.
He's getting too interested in some of the teams.
He's wanting winners and losers, and he's losing
Simple solidarity with the truth.
There's a lesson here,' I thought, as I watched
His week-by-week collapse to the haphazard,

Juggling hopes and fantasy, human and anxious.
He preferred to talk about poetry. He made poems.
He spelled one out:
                    'Nameless he shall be
The myriad of daughters
Tending his image
Washing the mountain slopes with tears
To slake the parched plains'.
                              'Is that a good poem?'
I asked him. 'That poem', he declared,
'Is a great poem.' His favourite poet
Was Shakespeare. His favourite poem *King Lear.*
And his favourite line in *King Lear?* 'Never
Never never never never' – but
He could not remember what followed.
We remembered but he could not remember.
When we pressed him he circled, baffled, then:
'Why shall I ever be perplexed thus?
I'd hack my arm off like a rotten branch
Had it betrayed me as my memory.'
Where did he find that? Or did he invent it?
It was an odd joke. He liked jokes.
More often serious. Once, as we bent there, I asked:
'Shall we be famous?' and you snatched your hand upwards
As if something had grabbed it from under.
Your tears flashed, your face was contorted,
Your voice cracked, it was thunder and flash together:
'And give yourself to the glare? Is that what you want?
Why should you want to be famous?
Don't you see – fame will ruin everything.'
I was stunned. I thought I had joined
Your association of ambition
To please you and your mother,

To fulfil your mother's ambition
That we be ambitious. Otherwise
I'd be fishing off a rock
In Western Australia. So it seemed suddenly. You wept.
You wouldn't go on with Ouija. Nothing
I could think of could explain
Your shock and crying. Only
Maybe you'd picked up a whisper I could not hear,
Before our glass could stir, some still small voice:
'Fame will come. Fame especially for you.
Fame cannot be avoided. And when it comes
You will have paid for it with your happiness,
Your husband and your life.'

The Earthenware Head

Who modelled your head of terracotta?
Some American student friend.
Life-size, the lips half-pursed, raw-edged
With crusty tooling – a naturalistic attempt
At a likeness that just failed. You did not like it.
I did not like it. Unease magnetized it
For a perverse rite. What possessed us
To take it with us, in your red bucket bag?
November fen-damp haze, the river unfurling
Dark whorls, ferrying slender willow yellows.
The pollard willows wore comfortless antlers,
Switch-horns, leafless. Just past where the field
Broadens and the path strays up to the right
To lose the river and puzzle for Grantchester,
A chosen willow leaned towards the water.
Above head height, the socket of a healed bole-wound,
A twiggy crotch, nearly an owl's porch,
Made a mythic shrine for your double.
I fitted it upright, firm. And a willow tree
Was a Herm, with your head, watching East
Through those tool-stabbed pupils. We left it
To live the world's life and weather for ever.

You ransacked thesaurus in your poem about it,
Veiling its mirror, rhyming yourself into safety
From its orphaned fate.
But it would not leave you. Weeks later
We could not seem to hit on the tree. We did not
Look too hard – just in passing. Already
You did not want to fear, if it had gone,

What witchcraft might ponder it. You never
Said much more about it.
                              What happened?
Maybe nothing happened. Perhaps
It is still there, representing you
To the sunrise, and happy
In its cold pastoral, lips pursed slightly
As if my touch had only just left it.
Or did boys find it – and shatter it? Or
Did the tree too kneel finally?

Surely the river got it. Surely
The river is its chapel. And keeps it. Surely
Your deathless head, fired in a furnace,
Face to face at last, kisses the Father
Mudded at the bottom of the Cam,
Beyond recognition or rescue,
All our fears washed from it, and perfect,
Under the stained mournful flow, saluted
Only in summer briefly by the slender
Punt-loads of shadows flitting towards their honey
And the stopped clock.
                              Evil.
That was what you called the head. Evil.

Wuthering Heights

Walter was guide. His mother's cousin
Inherited some Brontë soup dishes.
He felt sorry for them. Writers
Were pathetic people. Hiding from it
And making it up. But your transatlantic elation
Elated him. He effervesced
Like his rhubarb wine kept a bit too long:
A vintage of legends and gossip
About those poor lasses. Then,
After the Rectory, after the chaise longue
Where Emily died, and the midget hand-made books,
The elvish lacework, the dwarfish fairy-work shoes,
It was the track from Stanbury. That climb
A mile beyond expectation, into
Emily's private Eden. The moor
Lifted and opened its dark flower
For you too. That was satisfactory.
Wilder, maybe, than ever Emily knew it.
With wet feet and nothing on her head
She trudged that climbing side towards friends –
Probably. Dark redoubt
On the skyline above. It was all
Novel and exhilarating to you.
The book becoming a map. *Wuthering Heights*
Withering into perspective. We got there
And it was all gaze. The open moor,
Gamma rays and decomposing starlight
Had repossessed it
With a kind of blackening smoulder. The centuries
Of door-bolted comfort finally amounted
To a forsaken quarry. The roofs'

Deadfall slabs were flaking, but mostly in place,
Beams and purlins softening. So hard
To imagine the life that had lit
Such a sodden, raw-stone cramp of refuge.
The floors were a rubble of stone and sheep droppings.
Doorframes, windowframes –
Gone to make picnickers' fires or evaporated.
Only the stonework – black. The sky – blue.
And the moor-wind flickering.

                        The incomings,
The outgoings – how would you take up now
The clench of that struggle? The leakage
Of earnings off a few sickly bullocks
And a scatter of crazed sheep. Being cornered
Kept folk here. Was that crumble of wall
Remembering a try at a garden? Two trees
Planted for company, for a child to play under,
And to have something to stare at. Sycamores –
The girth and spread of valley twenty-year-olds,
They were probably ninety.

                      You breathed it all in
With jealous, emulous sniffings. Weren't you
Twice as ambitious as Emily? Odd
To watch you, such a brisk pendant
Of your globe-circling aspirations,
Among those burned-out, worn-out remains
Of failed efforts, failed hopes –
Iron beliefs, iron necessities,
Iron bondage, already
Crumbling back to the wild stone.

                      You perched
In one of the two trees
Just where the snapshot shows you.

Doing as Emily never did. You
Had all the liberties, having life.
The future had invested in you –
As you might say of a jewel
So brilliantly faceted, refracting
Every tint, where Emily had stared
Like a dying prisoner.
And a poem unfurled from you
Like a loose frond of hair from your nape
To be clipped and kept in a book. What would stern
Dour Emily have made of your frisky glances
And your huge hope? Your huge
Mortgage of hope. The moor-wind
Came with its empty eyes to look at you,
And the clouds gazed sidelong, going elsewhere,
The heath-grass, fidgeting in its fever,
Took idiot notice of you. And the stone,
Reaching to touch your hand, found you real
And warm, and lucent, like that earlier one.
And maybe a ghost, trying to hear your words,
Peered from the broken mullions
And was stilled. Or was suddenly aflame
With the scorch of doubled envy. Only
Gradually quenched in understanding.

The Chipmunk

A rippling, bobbing wood-elf, the chipmunk came
Under the Cape Cod conifers, over roots,
A first scout of the continent's wild game,
Midget aboriginal American. Flowing
On electrical accurate feet
Through its circuitry. That was the first real native –
Dodging from flashlit listening still
To staring flashlit still. It studied me
Sitting at a book – a strange prisoner,
Pacing my priceless years away, eyes lowered,
To and fro, to and fro,
Across my page. It snapped a tail-gesture at me –
Roused me, peremptory, to this friendship
It would be sharing with me
Only a few more seconds.
                              Its eyes
Popping with inky joy,
Globed me in a new vision, woke me,
And I recognized it.
                              You stayed
Alien to me as a window model,
American, airport-hopping superproduct,
Through all our intimate weeks up to the moment,
In a flash-still, retorting to my something,
You made a chipmunk face. I thought
An eight-year-old child was suddenly a chipmunk.
Pursed mouth, puffed cheeks. And suddenly,
Just in that flash – as I laughed
And got my snapshot for life,

And shouted: 'That's my first ever real chipmunk!' –
A ghost, dim, a woodland spirit, swore me
To take his orphan.

Horoscope

You wanted to study
Your stars – the guards
Of your prison yard, their zodiac. The planets
Muttered their Babylonish power-sprach –
Like a witchdoctor's bones. You were right to fear
How loud the bones might roar,
How clear an ear might hear
What the bones whispered
Even embedded as they were in the hot body.

Only you had no need to calculate
Degrees for your ascendant disruptor
In Aries. It meant nothing certain – no more
According to the Babylonian book
Than a scarred face. How much deeper
Under the skin could any magician peep?

You only had to look
Into the nearest face of a metaphor
Picked out of your wardrobe or off your plate
Or out of the sun or the moon or the yew tree
To see your father, your mother, or me
Bringing you your whole Fate.

[64]

Flounders

Was that a happy day? From Chatham
Down at the South end of the Cape, our map
Somebody's optimistic assurance,
We set out to row. We got ourselves
Into mid-channel. The tide was flowing. We hung
Anchored. Northward-pulling, our baited leads
Bounced and bounced the bottom. For three hours –
Two or three sea-robins. Cruisers
Folded us under their bow-waves, we bobbed up,
Happy enough. But the wind
Smartened against us, and the tide turned, roughening,
Dragged seaward. We rowed. We rowed. We
Saw we weren't going to make it. We turned,
Cutting downwind for the sand-bar, beached
And wondered what next. It was there
I found a horse-shoe crab's carapace, perfect,
No bigger than a bee, in honey-pale cellophane.
No way back. But big, good America found us.
A power-boat and a pilot of no problems.
He roped our boat to his stern and with all his family
Slammed back across the channel into the wind,
The spray scything upwards, our boat behind
Twisting across the wake-boil – a hectic
Four or five minutes and he cast us off
In the lee of the land, but a mile or more
From our dock. We toiled along inshore. We came
To a back-channel, under beach-house gardens – marsh grass,
Wild, original greenery of America,
Mud-slicks and fiddler-crab warrens, as we groped
Towards the harbour. Gloom-rich water. Something
Suggested easy plenty. We lowered baits,

And out of about six feet of water
Six or seven feet from land, we pulled up flounders
Big as big plates, till all our bait had gone.
After our wind-burned, head-glitter day of emptiness,
And the slogging row for our lives, and the rescue,
Suddenly out of water easy as oil
The sea piled our boat with its surplus. And the day
Curled out of brilliant, arduous morning,
Through wind-hammered perilous afternoon,
Salt-scoured, to a storm-gold evening, a luxury
Of rowing among the dream-yachts of the rich
Lolling at anchor off the play-world pier.

How tiny an adventure
To stay so monumental in our marriage,
A slight ordeal of all that might be,
And a small thrill-breath of what many live by,
And a small prize, a toy miniature
Of the life that might have bonded us
Into a single animal, a single soul –

It was a visit from the goddess, the beauty
Who was poetry's sister – she had come
To tell poetry she was spoiling us.
Poetry listened, maybe, but we heard nothing
And poetry did not tell us. And we
Only did what poetry told us to do.

The Blue Flannel Suit

I had let it all grow. I had supposed
It was all OK. Your life
Was a liner I voyaged in.
Costly education had fitted you out.
Financiers and committees and consultants
Effaced themselves in the gleam of your finish.
You trembled with the new life of those engines.

That first morning,
Before your first class at College, you sat there
Sipping coffee. Now I know, as I did not,
What eyes waited at the back of the class
To check your first professional performance
Against their expectations. What assessors
Waited to see you justify the cost
And redeem their gamble. What a furnace
Of eyes waited to prove your metal. I watched
The strange dummy stiffness, the misery,
Of your blue flannel suit, its straitjacket, ugly
Half-approximation to your idea
Of the proprieties you hoped to ease into,
And your horror in it. And the tanned
Almost green undertinge of your face
Shrunk to its wick, your scar lumpish, your plaited
Head pathetically tiny.
                     You waited,
Knowing yourself helpless in the tweezers
Of the life that judged you, and I saw
The flayed nerve, the unhealable face-wound
Which was all you had for courage.
I saw that what gripped you, as you sipped,

[67]

Were terrors that had killed you once already.
Now, I see, I saw, sitting, the lonely
Girl who was going to die.
                              That blue suit,
A mad, execution uniform,
Survived your sentence. But then I sat, stilled,
Unable to fathom what stilled you
As I looked at you, as I am stilled
Permanently now, permanently
Bending so briefly at your open coffin.

Child's Park

What did they mean to you, the azalea flowers?
Those girls were so happy, rending the branches,
Embracing their daring bouquets, their sumptuous
    trousseaux,
The wet, hot-petalled blossoms. Seizing their day,
Having a good time. Your homicidal
Hooded stare met them head on.
As if they were stealing the brands
Of your own burning. I hurried you off. Bullfrogs
Took you down through lily tangle. Your fury
Had to be quenched. Heavy water,
Deeper, deeper, cooling and controlling
Your plutonium secret. You breathed water.

Freed, steadied, resurfaced, your eyes
Alit afresh on colour, so delicate,
Splitting the prism,
As the dragonflies on the solid lilies.
The pileated woodpecker went writhing
Among the catalpas. It clung
To undersides and swooped
Like a pterodactyl. The devilry
Of the uncoiling head, the spooky wings,
And the livid cry
Flung the garden open.
                              You were never
More than a step from Paradise.
You had instant access, your analyst told you,
To the core of your Inferno –
The pit of the hairy flower.
                              At a sunny angle

The fountain threw off its seven veils
As the air swayed it. Here was your stair –
Alchemy's seven colours.
I watched you as you climbed it all on your own
Into the mouth of the azalea.

You imagined a veil-rending defloration
And a rebirth out of the sun – mixed up together
And somehow the same. You were fearless
To meet your Father,
His Word fulfilled, there, in the nuclear core.

What happens in the heart simply happens.

I stepped back. That glare
Flinging your old selves off like underthings
Left your whole Eden radioactive.

9 Willow Street

Willow Street, poetical address.
Number nine, even better. It confirmed
We had to have it. We got it.
A tower of the Muses. Freed from school
For the first time in your life, this was the cage
Your freedom flew to – a view of the Charles River
And Cambridge beyond it. Over my table
I covered the windows with brown paper,
Pushed ear-plugs in on my inflamed nerves
And sank. In the other room,
Perched up in the glare, on the cliff-edge,
You hammered your new Hermes,
Your Panic Bird chipping at the old egg,
While I rolled in my sack, with my lumber,
Along the bottom of the Charles. We huddled. Me
In my black sack striking sulphur matches
To find the eyes of Jung's nigredo. You
In a paralysis of terror-flutters
I hardly understood. I folded
Black wings round you, wings of the blackness
That enclosed me, rocking me, infantile,
And enclosed you with me. And your heart
Jumped at your ribs, you gasped for air.
You grabbed for the world,
For straws, for your morning coffee – anything
To get airborne. My bubbles
Wobbled upwards and burst emptily
In the reverberations of the turbines
Home and College had assembled in you,

That thundered the parquet
And shook you to tremblings. Your day
Was twenty-four rungs of a fire-escape
Hanging in ghastly swirls, over nothing,
Reaching up towards nothing.
What an airy Hell!

                        Boston clanged
All its atoms below, through all its circles
Between Harvard and Scollay Square. Alone
Either of us might have met with a life.
Siamese-twinned, each of us festering
A unique soul-sepsis for the other,
Each of us was the stake
Impaling the other. We struggled
Quietly through the streets, affirming each other,
Dream-maimed and dream-blind.

                                    Your typewriter,
Your alarm clock, your new sentence
Tortured you, a cruelty computer
Of agony niceties, daily afresh –
Every letter a needle, as in Kafka.
While I, like a poltergeist fog,
Hung on you, fed on you – heavy, drugged
With your nightmares and terrors. Inside your Bell Jar
I was like a mannikin in your eyeball.
What happened casually remains –
Strobes of a hallucinating fever
In some heaving dimension of chemical horror.
Our only escape was into arms
That reached upwards or reached downwards
And rolled us all night eastward with each other

Over the bottom, in the muddy current.
What a waste!
What did our spectre-blinded searching reach
Or wake to, that was worth it?

                         Happiness

Appeared – momentary,
Peered in at your window
Like a wild migrant, an oriole,
A tanager, a humming-bird – pure American,
Blown scraps of the continent's freedom –
But off course and gone
Before we could identify it.

It took me a dizzy moment to make out
Something under the chestnuts, struggling
On a path of the Common, down near the Swan-boats.
What looked like a slug, black, soft, wrinkled,
Was wrestling, somehow, with the fallen
Brown, crumpled lobe of a chestnut leaf.
Suddenly, plainly, it was a bat.
A bat fallen out of its tree
Mid-afternoon. A sick bat? I stooped
Thinking I'd lift it again to tree-bark safety.
It reared up on its elbows and snarled at me,
A raving hyena, the size of a sparrow,
Its whole face peeled in a snarl, fangs tiny.
I tried to snatch it up by the shoulders
But it spun, like a fighter, behind its snarl.

A crowd collected, entertained to watch me
Fight a bat on Boston Common. Finally
I had to give it my finger.
Let the bite lock. Then, cradling it,

Gently lifted it and offered it up
To the wall of chestnut bark. It released me
And scuttled upwards backwards, face downwards,
A rearguard snarl, triumphant, contorted,
Vanishing upwards into where it had come from.

At home I looked at the blood, and remembered:
American bats have rabies. How could Fate
Stage a scenario so symbolic
Without having secreted the tragedy ending
And the ironic death? It confirmed
The myth we had sleepwalked into: death.
This was the bat-light we were living in: death.

The Literary Life

We climbed Marianne Moore's narrow stair
To her bower-bird bric-à-brac nest, in Brooklyn.
Daintiest curio relic of Americana.
Her talk, a needle
Unresting – darning incessantly
Chain-mail with crewel-work flowers,
Birds and fish of the reef
In phosphor-bronze wire.
Her face, tiny American treen bobbin
On a spindle,
Her voice the flickering hum of the old wheel.
Then the coin, compulsory,
For the subway
Back to our quotidian scramble.
Why shouldn't we cherish her?

You sent her carbon copies of some of your poems.
Everything about them –
The ghost gloom, the constriction,
The bell-jar air-conditioning – made her gasp
For oxygen and cheer. She sent them back.
(Whoever has her letter has her exact words.)
'Since these seem to be valuable carbon copies
(Somewhat smudged) I shall not engross them.'
I took the point of that 'engross'
Precisely, like a bristle of glass
Snapped off deep in my thumb.
You wept
And hurled yourself down a floor or two
Further from the Empyrean.
I carried you back up.

[75]

And she, Marianne, tight, brisk,
Neat and hard as an ant,
Slid into the second or third circle
Of my Inferno.

A decade later, on her last visit to England,
Holding court at a party, she was sitting
Bowed over her knees, her face,
Under her great hat-brim's floppy petal,
Dainty and bright as a piece of confetti –
She wanted me to know, she insisted
(It was all she wanted to say)
With that Missouri needle, drawing each stitch
Tight in my ear,
That your little near-posthumous memoir
'OCEAN 1212'
Was 'so wonderful, so lit, so wonderful' –

She bowed so low I had to kneel. I kneeled and
Bowed my face close to her upturned face
That seemed tinier than ever,
And studied, as through a grille,
Her lips that put me in mind of a child's purse
Made of the skin of a dormouse,
Her cheek, as if she had powdered the crumpled silk
Of a bat's wing.
And I listened, heavy as a graveyard
While she searched for the grave
Where she could lay down her little wreath.

The Bird

Under its glass dome, behind its eyes,
Your Panic Bird was not stuffed. It was looking
For you did not know what. I could feel
For the glass – not there and yet there –
A zoo gecko glued against nothing
With all its life throbbing in its throat,
As if it stood on ether. The Princess
Let her hair right down to the ground
From her solitary high window. Remember,
Circling Boston Common together,
The defective jailbird walk we perfected,
Feet swinging from the knees. A Tyrolean
Clockwork, revolving under glass,
To a tinkling. You told me
Everything but the fairy tale. Step for step
I walked in the sleep
You tried to wake from.

                      You widened your pupils
For thunderclap dawn – at the wharf,
And in came that ice-caked ship,
Fretworked chandelier of lacy crystals,
A whole wedding vessel lifted from under
The ocean salt – flash-frozen. Then you turned,
Your eyelashes clogged, and stretched your eyes
At the charred-out caves of apartment block
That had burned all night, a flame-race upwards
Under the hoses, behind the Senate. You howled
With your sound turned off and your screen dark
For tragedy to go on – to hell with the curtain.
You willed it to get going all over again,
Spit one spark of woe through the frozen suds

That draped the gutted building
Like a solid Niagara.

What glowed into focus was blood suddenly
Weltering dumb and alive
Up through the tattooed blazon of an eagle.
Your homeland's double totem. Germany's eagle
Bleeding up through your American eagle
In a cloud of Dettol. It jabbed
Its talons at the glass. It wanted
To be born, pecking at the glass. Tears were no good.
Though you could smash a mahogany heirloom table
With a high stool for an axe,
Tears were rain on a window.

We stood married, in a packed room, drinking sherry,
In some Cambridge College. My eyes
Had locked on a chunky tumbler
Solid with coins (donations to pay for the booze),
Isolated on a polished table.
I was staring at it when it vanished
Like a spinning grenade, with a bang.
The coins collapsed in a slither. But the table
Was suddenly white with a shatter of tiny crystals.
A cake of frozen snow
Could have crashed in from space. Every crumb
Of smithereen that I peered into
Was flawed into crystals infinitely tiny

Like crumbs of the old, slabbed snow
That all but barricaded London
The day your bird broke free and the glass dome
Vanished – with a ringing sound

I thought was a telephone.
I knew the glass had gone and the bird had gone.
Like lifting an eyelid I peered for the glass –
But I knew it had gone. Because of the huge
Loose emptiness of light
Wheeling through everything.
As if a gecko
Fell into empty light.

Astringency

I always think of the Charles River
Frozen. The word 'Astringency'
Was the cant for years.
Slackly I strolled there. A big event:
A million dead worms
Littering the lawny grass along the walkway.
Modern times had caught them up
And overtaken. String ends
Too short to be saved. The cindery air,
A waft of roasted iron, blew from Cambridge.
'Lit Crit,' my friend said, 'and Agrochemicals
Are Siamese twins.' What? Were you with me
When I saw an amazing thing,
Right there at the edge of the Charles?
A fisherman, hoping for God knows what,
Had just caught a goldfish.
Out of that brown mass, from under
The hundred miles and the thousand false faces
Of the Charles River
That I had assumed 100 per cent proof toxic.
A goldfish! Thick, deep and very frisky.
Nine inches long – obviously thriving.
Somebody's apartment darling – flushed?
But caught again! Brainstorm of the odds!
He let it go. It swam off.
It dissolved in the murk. That same spot
We – you and me – watched small, ranked waves
Washing over a nipple of rock at the edge there.
You and me, standing on America,
Together, silent, thinking of nothing, watching
The sliding ring of ripple

That each small, tired wave threw over the rock
'Like a lariat,' you said.

The sole metaphor that ever escaped you
In easy speech, in my company –
Past the censor? Past the night hands?
Past the snare
Set in your throat by whom? Who caught all
That teeming population, every one,
To hang their tortured eyes and tongues up
In your poems? To what end? The constrictor
Not to be tugged out, or snapped.

The Badlands

Right across America
We went looking for you. Lightning
Had ripped your clothes off
And signed your cheekbone. It came
Out of the sun's explosion
Over Hiroshima, Nagasaki,
As along the ridge of a mountain
Under the earth, and somehow
Through death-row and the Rosenbergs.
They took the brunt of it.
You weren't too logical about it.
You only knew it had come and had gripped you
By the roots of the hair
And held you down on the bed
And stretched across your retina
The global map of nerves in blue flames,
Then left you signed and empty. But already
You had got clear –
Jumped right out of your crackling cast
Through that hole over your cheekbone
And gone to ground, gone underground, into moonland
Somewhere in America.
                              We came to a stone
Beside a lake flung open before dawn
By the laugh of a loon. The signs good,
I turned the stone over. The timeless one,
Head perfect, eyes waiting – there he lay.
Banded black,
White, black, white, coiled. I said:
'Just like the coils on the great New Grange lintel.'
One thing to find a guide,

Another to follow him.
                    In North Dakota
We met smoke of the underground burning –
A fistula of smouldering bitumen.
Hellish. Or lit by lightning. Or
Dante's, to coach us. Ignited
By the moon's collision. I saw it in a dream
Coming bigger and closer till almost
The size of the earth it crashed
Into the Atlantic –
I watched it from the point of Manhattan.
The earth took it with a tremendous jolt –
Impact and penetration. Next thing
The moon was inside the earth,
Cramming its phosphor flames
Under the scabby humped pelt of the prairies.
And above me the towers of Manhattan
Swayed like curtains of ash.
                    In the Badlands
We got deeper. A landscape
Staked out in the sun and left to die.
The Theodore Roosevelt National Park.
Long ago dead of the sun. Loose teeth, bone
Coming through crust, bristles.
Or a smashed industrial complex
For production
Of perpetual sacrifice, of canyons
Long ago disembowelled.
When Aztec and Inca went on South
They left the sun waiting,
Starved for worship, raging for attention,
Now gone sullenly mad.
As it sank it stared at our car.

[83]

Middle distance, yellow, the Missouri
Crawled, stagnated, crawled.

The silence, at least,
Like a cooling incinerator
Was an afterlife. As it cooled
Every clinker inched its shadow wider
And darker
Like a little door. There we camped.
The most inimical place I ever was in.
Too late to go on. I remember

A lone tree near the campsite.
I kept looking towards it –
For comfort? It gave none.
As we pitched our tent
You were uneasy. You kept being overwhelmed
By the misery of the place, like a nausea.
You kept having to stand up and look round.

We were tired.
Easy prey. We went for a walk.
Everything watched us. We stood, not chilled yet,
Watching the sun go –
A half, a quarter, as if it were being drained.
Then all gone.
                    At that moment something
Heaved out of the land and was there.
Empty, horrible, archaic – America.
Planetary – before the eye touched it.
A land with maybe one idea – snake.

But then, suddenly, near us
Something hectic in a rickety thorn-bush.
It was a tiny terror, a maniac midget
Hurtling in top-gear uncontrol –
Like a ball on a pin-table, clash and ricochet,
Terror bounce and back, clash and back,
Through the maze of the thorn-bush. I thought
A panicky bird, fluttering maybe tethered
By a slim snake like a bootlace
Couldn't break out of the thorns. I thought
Some electrical predator hunted
Electrical tiny prey. Or two
Tiny birds of desert ferocity
Fought in there. It was a solitary mouse.

Somewhere in that iron-hearth, ashen landscape
He had found dewdrops enough for his eyes
And was protecting them – with an energy
More like torturing poison
Than what could be found in food. Where was his food?
And what was he doing here
In this solar furnace
Of oxides and firedust?
And what was he up to in his gymnasium,
All on his own, burning up calories,
Blazing off nervous tension, having a breakdown –
Overloaded with emergency fury
Or some uncontainable surplus of joy?
He skittered about his flimsy
Castle of spines, dodging maybe
The deadly radiation of our attention
As we peered in from the sky – and

He'd vanished. His scatter of intricate racket
Went on some seconds after him.

The canyons cooled. Indigo darkened,
Oozing out of the earth like ectoplasm,
A huge snake heaping out. 'This is evil,'
You said. 'This is real evil.'
Whatever it was, the whole landscape wore it
Like a plated mask. 'What is it?'
I kept saying. 'What is it?'
As if that might force the whatever
To materialize, maybe standing by our car,
Maybe some old Indian.
                                        'Maybe it's the earth,'
You said. 'Or maybe it's ourselves.
This emptiness is sucking something out of us.
Here where there's only death, maybe our life
Is terrifying. Maybe it's the life
In us
Frightening the earth, and frightening us.'

Fishing Bridge

Nearly happy. Brilliantly lit –
That threshold of the great lake
Spilling its river. Naive pioneers,
We had no idea what we were seeing
When we watched the cut-throat beneath our boat,
Marching, massed, over the sunken threshold
Of the Yellowstone.
                                    Petty precautions
To keep our skulls clear of the whizzing leads
Catapulted from the lashing rods
Of the holiday anglers – a cram of colour
Along the bank and the bridge – took all our forethought.
We did not see what infinite endowment
Leaned over that threshold, beckoning us
With that glitter of distance as it gathered
The trout into its bounty.
                                    Little finesse,
With bumping leads and earthworms. No problem
Catching our limit dozen
Of those weary migrants, pushing and pushed
Towards their spawning gravels. What I remember
Is the sun's dazzle – and your delight
Wandering off along the lake's fringe
Towards the shag-headed wilderness
In your bikini. There you nearly
Stepped into America. You turned back,
And we turned away. That lake-mouth
Was only one of too many thresholds –

Every one of them a glittering offer.
We half-closed our eyes. Or held them wide

Like sleepwalkers while a voice on a tape,
Promising, directed us into a doorway
Difficult and dark. The voice urged on
Into an unlit maze of crying and loss.
What voice? 'Find your souls,' said the voice.
'Find your true selves. This way. Search, search.'
The voice had never heard of the shining lake.
'Find the core of the labyrinth.' Why? What opens
At the heart of the maze? Is it the doorway
Into the perfected vision? Masterfully
The voice pushed us, hypnotized, bowing our heads
Into its dead-ends, its reversals,
Dreamy gropings, baffled ponderings,
Its monomaniac half-search, half-struggle,
Not for the future – not for any future –

Till it stopped. Was that the maze's centre?
Where everything stopped? What lay there?
The voice held me there, by the scruff of the neck,
And bowed my head
Over the thing we had found. Your dead face.
Your dead lips, dry, pale. And your eyes
(As brown-bright, when I lifted the lids,
As when you gazed across that incandescence)
Unmoving and dead.

The 59th Bear

We counted bears – as if all we wanted
Were more bears. Yellowstone
Folded us into its robe, its tepees
Of mountain and conifer.
Mislaid Red Indian Mickey Mouse America
Pointered us from campground to campground –
We were two of many. And it was as novel-astonishing
To you as to me. Paradise, we saw,
Was where wild bears ate from the hands of children.
Were these real wild bears? We saw Daddies
Supporting their babies piggyback on dark bears
In a dancing ring of guffaws and cameras.
The bears were in on the all-American family,
Originals of those board cut-out bears,
Uncle Bruins in Disneyland overalls,
Who warned against forest fires. Bears waited –
Welcoming committees – at every parking,
Lifting their teddybear ears and quizzing buttons
At the car windows. Twenty, we counted.
Thirty. Forty. Fifty. Once
As I opened the car door at a café
A bear that just happened to be passing
Shouldered it shut.
Everywhere people were entertaining
Bears and bears were entertaining people.

We roamed, soon at home in the marvellous abundance.
Eagles were laid on too. We leaned at a rail
And looked down onto floating black flecks
That turned out to be eagles – we were swept
Into the general exclamatory joy

By somebody's binoculars. I stared
Down through the spread fingers of an eagle
Into a drop that still scares me to remember.
But it all refused to be translated.
The Camp Ranger notices seemed perfunctory,
Make-believe. Through coy nicknames magma
Bubbled its colours, belched its labouring sighs –
Prehistory was still at boiling point,
Smoking round us.
                    Each evening
Bears raided the campgrounds. Camera stars,
They performed at the sunken trash-bins. Delight –
Every few days a whole new class of campers
Squealing for fearless close-ups before
The warnings sank in.
                        Somehow that night
The warnings had sunk in. You were nervous.
It had been a day of worsening nerves.
We had driven just too far. The gas
Had got too low and the evening too late.

Your spirits as usual had gone right down with
The fuel-gauge to the bottom, and bobbed there –
You saw us in a vision, a headline,
Devoured in the night-woods. One curve in the road
Became dreadful – nearly impassable.
A giant elk detached itself abruptly
From the conifer black, wheeled its rigging
Right above the bonnet and vanished, like a sign
From some place of omens. We reached our tent
In the dusk of campfires.
                            Three cold fried trout
Were surplus from breakfast. But

It was too late to sit up under the stars
Sipping and eating – 'The bears!' The bears were coming!
With a racket of clatter-pans, and a yelling
From the far end of the campground – 'Bears! Bears!' –
You panicked into the tent and pleaded.
I saw a big brown bear and a smaller, darker,
Romping like big rubber toys,
Bouncing along, like jolly inflatables
Among the tents and tables. Awesome, fluid,
Unpredictable, dodging swiftness! And cries.
The whole campground was jumpy – a cacophony
Of bangings and shouts urging the bears
On and away elsewhere – anywhere away
Pestering somebody else. I locked everything
Into the car. Each thing carefully checked.
One thing I missed.
                    Did we sleep?
The campground slept. The bears had been scared off,
To other campgrounds. How safe we felt
In our green breathing walls! Hidden breathers,
Safe and chrysalis in our sleeping bags,
Trusting each moment to elide into another
As quiet as itself. Vast, bristling darkness
Of America. Under my pillow –
Drastic resource for a drastic emergency –
I kept the hatchet, purposefully sharpened.

What time was it? A rending crash – too close –
Had me head up and alert, listening,
As if I watched what made it. Then more rendings
Of real awful damage going on,
Still being done – and you were awake too,
Listening beside me. I got up

And peered through the tent's window mesh into moonlight.
Everything clear, black-shadowed. The car
Five paces away, looked natural enough.
Then more rippings inside it, and it shook,
And I saw the dark blockage, a black mass
Filling the far rear window. 'Those damned bears!
One's getting into the car.'
                                    A few shock-shouts,
I thought, a close-up assault of human abuse,
And the bear would be off. I'd take my hatchet
Just in case. I got out my hatchet,
Pitifully unimaginative.
I was remembering those amiable bears.
That's how it happens. Your terrors
Were more intelligent, with their vision –
And I was not so sure. Then for an hour
He was unpacking the car, unpuzzling our bags,
Raking and thumping. I imagined
Every scrap of fabric ripped from the springs.
It sounded like a demolition. We lay
Decoding every variety of sound
As he battered and squelched, crunched and scraped
With still intervals of meditation.
I got up again. In first faint light
I made him out wrestling our steel freezer
Between his paws. 'It's the big brown one.' We'd heard
He was the nasty one. Again we lay quiet,
Letting him do what he wanted.
                                    And at last
A new sound – the caress, ushering closer,
The lullaby reveille of a cruising engine:
The Camp Ranger's car, doing the dawn rounds.
The bear heard it. And we had the joy –

Awful incredulity like joy –
Of hearing his claw-bunches hurry-scuffle
To the secret side of our tent. He was actually there,
Hiding beside our tent! His breathing,
Heavy after the night's gourmandizing,
Rasped close to the canvas – only inches
From your face that, big-eyed, stared at me
Staring at you.
                    The car cruised easily away
Into the forest and lake silence. The bear
Faded from his place, as the tent walls paled.
Loons on the glassed lake shook off their nightmares.
The day came.
                    A ghoul had left us,
Leaving our freezer buckled open, our fish
Vanished from their stains, every orange
Sucked flat, our pancake mix
Dabbled over yards of dust, everything
Edible gone, in a scatter of wrappers
And burst cartons. And the off rear window of the car
Wrenched out – a star of shatter splayed
From a single talon's leverage hold,
A single claw forced into the hair-breadth odour
Had ripped the whole sheet out. He'd leaned in
And on claw hooks lifted out our larder.
He'd left matted hairs. I glued them in my Shakespeare.

I felt slightly dazed – a strange pride
To have been so chosen and ego-raked
By the deliberations of that beast.

But you came back from the wash-house
With your last-night's panic double-boosted

For instant flight.
                    Some doppelgänger,
That very night, at the next campground,
Had come out of his tent to shoo off a bear
With a torch and a few shouts. He'd learned –
Briefly, in what flash of reckoning
He'd been allowed – what I had hardly guessed:
A bear's talons, which by human flesh
Can be considered steel, braced on tendons
Of steel hawser, are on the end of an arm
That can weigh sixty, seventy, eighty pounds
Moving at 90 m.p.h.
Your terror had the mathematics perfect.
You had met a woman in the wash-house
Who'd driven terrified from that other campground.
And you just knew, it was that very same bear.
Having murdered a man, he'd romped through the woods
To rob us.
That was our fifty-ninth bear. I saw, well enough,
The peril that see-saws opposite
A curious impulse – what slight flicker
In a beast's brain electrifies tonnage
And turns life to paper. I did not see
What flicker in yours, what need later
Transformed our dud scenario into a fiction –
Or what self-salvation
Squeezed the possible blood out of it
Through your typewriter ribbon.
                              At that time

I had not understood
How the death hurtling to and fro
Inside your head, had to alight somewhere
And again somewhere, and had to be kept moving,

[94]

And had to be rested
Temporarily somewhere.

Grand Canyon

Not a brimming glass of orange juice –
But you were suddenly more than careful
Not to spill a drop. There on the rim,
Watching the mules tilt down
Was almost nausea.
Miles off, opposite, the miles-high rampart cliff.
Miles below, the unshaved, two-day bristle
Was an eighty-foot ponderosa.
So they said. And the heat down there was hellish.

Too vast to be visible in,
A quarry from which the sculpture
Of something
Had been hacked, then left there
Too big to move.
America's big red mamma!
Now letting the sun, with changing colours,
Caress her, as she lay open.
We drifted our gaze through – like a feather
Lost in the afterglow of her sensations.

Six weeks pregnant and you were scared of the mules.
Yet here was the oracle.
This was America's Delphi. You wanted a sign.
We settled for the cougar-hunter. Scrawny,
Cantankerous old-timer. Stagey tales of the early canyon.
He showed slides without a joke.
Made his bag of five hundred lions
Sound as likely as finished.
You took against him
Even as his words played at your eardrums

And rippled their faint, canyon thunder
And lightning over her foetus.

We'd brought our water-cooler bag through the cinders of
    the Mojave.
Slung under the front bumper, au fait.
We seemed to be saving it. We still hadn't broached it.
We were stoned
With the heaped-up coils of highway crammed in our heads,
The mountains, the forests, the cities, the boysenberry pies
Jammed in our body-sacks. We were numbed by the shock-
    waves
Coming off the sky-vistas at us –
The thunder-beings that swept against us and through us
Out of the road's jackrabbits and the beer-can constellations
We drove into after dark.

We had sweated the labour, the pilgrimage.
Now we wanted the blessing.
Some word – from before this translation
Of the canyon lion to the dollar eagle.
We had big hope the Navajo dancers
Up there on their platform would deliver it.

PAUM! It came
The first thud of that drum
Before a single dancer popped up.

PAUM! The gorge spoke
Through that membrane,
The first summons
Out of its vertigo and nausea.

And every hair on my body
Jumped as if it were old dust on a drumskin.

PAUM!
Swallowed the whole memory,
The dancers, the crowd, the cameras, everything there on
  the canyon rim
Swallowed by a solitary thud.
You, me, and her – suspended
In her quaking echo-chamber – swallowed
As a bad accident
Wipes the memory just before and after –
The whole scene gone
Into *PAUM!*

I made a note so I know
We sleepwalked back to the car and found our water-bag
  stolen.

Nothing is left. I never went back and you are dead.
But at odd moments it comes,
As if for the first time, like a hand grabbing
And shaking me from light sleep,
Through all these years, and after thirty years,
Close, itself, ours as the voice of your daughter –

PAUM!

Karlsbad Caverns

We had seen the bats in the Karlsbad caves,
Thick as shaggy soot in chimneys
Bigger than cathedrals. We'd made ourselves dots

On the horizon of their complete world
And their exclusive lives.
Presumably the whole lot were happy –

So happy they didn't know they were happy,
They were so busy with it, so full of it,
Clinging upside down in their stone heavens.

Then we checked our watches. The vanguard bats,
To the minute, started to flicker and whirl
In the giant mouth of the cavern

That was our amphitheatre, where they were the drama.
A flickering few thickened to a million
Till critical boiling mass tore free of the magnet

Under the earth. The bats began to hurl out –
Spill out, smoke out, billow out,
For half an hour was it, an upward torrent

Of various millions of bats. A smoky dragon
Out of a key-hole in earth,
A great sky-snake writhing away southwards

Towards the Rio Grande
Where every night they caught their tons of insects –
Five tons, somebody said.

[99]

And that was how it should be.
As every night for how many million years?
A clockwork, perfected like their radar.

We weren't sure whether to stay that night or go.
We were where we had never been in our lives.
Visitors – visiting even ourselves.

The bats were part of the sun's machinery,
Connected to the machinery of the flowers
By the machinery of insects. The bats' meaning

Oiled the unfailing logic of the earth.
Cosmic requirement – on the wings of a goblin.
A rebuke to our flutter of half-participation.

Thoughts like that were stirring, when somebody yelled.
The sky-dragon of bats was making a knot.
'They're coming back!'
                        We stared and we saw,

Through the bats, a mushrooming range
Of top-heavy thunderheads, their shutters flashing
Over the Rio Grande. The bats had a problem.

Wings above their heads like folding umbrellas
They dived out of the height
Straight back into the cave – the whole cloud,

The vast ragged body of the genie
Pouring back into the phial. All over the South
The storm flashed and crawled like a war.

Those bats had their eyes open. Unlike us,
They knew how, and when, to detach themselves
From the love that moves the sun and the other stars.

Black Coat

I remember going out there,
The tide far out, the North Shore ice-wind
Cutting me back
To the quick of the blood – that outer-edge nostalgia,
The good feeling. My sole memory
Of my black overcoat. Padding the wet sandspit.
I was staring at the sea, I suppose.
Trying to feel thoroughly alone,
Simply myself, with sharp edges –
Me and the sea one big tabula rasa,
As if my returning footprints
Out of that scrim of gleam, that horizon-wide wipe,
Might be a whole new start.

My shoe-sole shapes
My only sign.
My minimal but satisfying discussion
With the sea.
Putting my remarks down, for the thin tongue
Of the sea to interpret. Inaudibly.
A therapy,
Instructions too complicated for me
At the moment, but stowed in my black box for later.
Like feeding a wild deer
With potato crisps
As you do in that snapshot where you exclaim
Back towards me and my camera.

So I had no idea I had stepped
Into the telescopic sights
Of the paparazzo sniper

Nested in your brown iris.
Perhaps you had no idea either,
So far off, half a mile maybe,
Looking towards me. Watching me
Pin the sea's edge down.
No idea
How that double image,
Your eye's inbuilt double exposure
Which was the projection
Of your two-way heart's diplopic error,
The body of the ghost and me the blurred see-through
Came into single focus,
Sharp-edged, stark as a target,
Set up like a decoy
Against that freezing sea
From which your dead father had just crawled.

I did not feel
How, as your lenses tightened,
He slid into me.

Portraits

What happened to Howard's portrait of you?
I wanted that painting.
Spirits helped Howard. 'Sometimes
When I'm painting, I hear a voice, a woman's,
Calling *Howard, Howard* – faint, far-off,
Fading.'
           He got carried away
When he started feeding his colours
Into your image. He glowed
At his crucible, on its tripod.
How many sessions?
Yaddo fall. Woodstoves. Rain,
Rain, rain in the conifers. Tribal conflict
Of crows and their echoes. You deepened,
Molten, luminous, looking at us
From that window of Howard's vision of you.
Yourself lifted out of yourself
In a flaming of oils, your lips exact.

Suddenly – 'What's that? Who's that?'
Out of the gloomy neglected chamber behind you
Somebody had emerged, hunched, gloating at you,
Just behind your shoulder – a cowled
Humanoid of raggy shadows. Who?
Howard was surprised. He smiled at it.
'If I see it there, I paint it. I like it
When things like that happen. He just came.'

Came from where? Mystery smudge extra,
Stalking the glaze wetness
Of your new-fired idol brilliance.

I saw it with horrible premonition.
You were alone there, pregnant, unprotected
In some inaccessible dimension
Where that creature had you, now, to himself.
As if Howard's brush-strokes tethered you there
In a dark emptiness, a bait, an offering,
To bring up – not a man-eater, not a monster,
Not a demon – what? Who?
                                    We watched
A small snake swim out, questing
Over the greenhouse dust – a bronze prong
Glistening life, tentative and vital
As a snail's horn, lifting its flow
Magnetically towards – 'Beautiful!'
That's what I cried. 'Look, Howard, beautiful!
So intense it's hypnotic!' Howard laughed.
Snakes are snakes. 'You like it,' he said,
'Because it's evil. It's evil, so it thrills you.'

You made no comment. Hardly a week before –
Entranced, gnawing your lips, your fingers counting
The touches of your thumb, delicately
Untangling on your fingers a music
That only you could hear, you had sat there,
Bowed as over a baby,
Conjuring into its shrine, onto your page,
This thing's dead immortal doppelgänger.

Stubbing Wharfe

Between the canal and the river
We sat in the gummy dark bar.
Winter night rain. The black humped bridge and its cobbles
Sweating black, under lamps of drizzling yellow.
And the hillsides going straight up, the high woods,
Massed with tangled wintry wet, and the moorland
Almost closing above us. The shut-in
Sodden dreariness of the whole valley,
The hopeless old stone trap of it. Where shall we live?
That was the question, in the yellow-lit tap-room
Which was cold and empty. You having leapt
Like a thrown dice, flinging off
The sparkle of America, pioneer
In the wrong direction, sat weeping,
Homesick, exhausted, disappointed, pregnant.
Where could we start living? Italy? Spain?
The world was all before us. And around us
This gloomy memorial of a valley,
The fallen-in grave of its history,
A gorge of ruined mills and abandoned chapels,
The fouled nest of the Industrial Revolution
That had flown. The windows glittered black.
If this was the glamour of an English pub, it was horrible.
Like a bubble in the sunk *Titanic*.
Our flashing inter-continental sleeper
Had slammed into a gruesome, dead-end tunnel.
Where could we camp? The ideal home
Was trying to crawl
Up out of my Guinness. Where we sat,
Forty years before I was born
My drunken grandad, dragged out of the canal,

Had sat in a sheet singing. A house of our own
Answering all your problems was the answer
To all my problems. All we needed
Was to get a home – anywhere,
Then all our goblins would turn out to be elves,
Our vampires guides, our demons angels
In that garden. Yes, the garden. The garden
Swelled under all our words – like the presence
Of what swelled in you.
                                        Everything
Was there in my Guinness. Where, exactly?
That was the question – that dark
Peculiar aftertaste, bitter liquorice
Of the secret ingredient. At that black moment
Prophecy, like a local owl,
Down from the deep-cut valley opposite
Made a circuit through its territory –
Your future and mine. 'These side-valleys,' I whispered,
'Are full of the most fantastic houses,
Elizabethan, marvellous, little kingdoms,
Going for next to nothing. For instance
Up there opposite – up that valley – '
My certainty of the place was visionary,
Waiting there, on its walled terrace – an eyrie
Over the crevasse of trees and water.
You had no idea what I was talking about.
Your eyes were elsewhere –
The sun-shot Atlantic lift, the thunderous beaches,
The ice-cream summits, the whisper of avalanches,
Valleys brimming gentians – the Lawrentian globe
Lit the crystal globe you stared into
For your future – while a silent
Wing of your grave went over you. Up that valley

A future home waited for both of us –
Two different homes. Where I saw so clearly
My vision house, you saw only blackness,
Black nothing, the face of nothingness,
Like that rainy window.
                              Then five bowlers
Burst in like a troupe of clowns, laughing.
They thumped down their bowls and ordered. Their star turn
Had a raging ulcer, agony.
Or the ulcer was the star. It kept
The five of them doubled up – tossing helpless
On fresh blasts of laughter. It stoked them
Like souls tossing in a hell, on a grill
Of helpless laughter, agony, tears
Streaming down their faces
Like sweat as they struggled, throats gulping,
To empty their glasses, refilling and emptying.
I had to smile. You had to smile. The future
Seemed to ease open a fraction.

Remission

A fragile cutting, tamped into earth,
You took root, you flourished only
In becoming fruitful – in getting pregnant,
In the oceanic submissions
Of giving birth. That was the you
You loved and wanted to live with.
The kernel of the shells – each prettily painted –
Of the doll from the Polish corridor,
The inmost, smiling, solid one, the joy-being,
Venus of Willendorf or the Wyf of Bath.

That was the you you shared with the wild earth.
It was your membership
Of a sorority of petals and creatures
Whose masonic signs are beauty and nectar
In the love-land, the Paradise
Your suicide had tried to drag you from.

And it was the you that escaped death
In the little woven vessel
On the most earthly river
Of that Paradise. Your Indian midwife
(Of all your fairy godmothers the timeliest,
For you she was a deity from the Ganges,
Black with alluvial wisdom) stroked your hair
And made you weep with relief, and stowed you aboard,
Folded you from yourself, lulled the passage
Of yourself from your bleeding self
With the face-mask of nitrous oxide that was empty,
With yoga breath,
With monkey-fine dark fingers delivered you

In a free-floating crib, an image that sneezed
And opened a gummed mouth and started to cry.
I was there, I saw it. As I helped you

Escape incognito
The death who had already donned your features,
The mask of his disguise.

Isis

The morning we set out to drive around America
She started with us. She was our lightest
Bit of luggage. And you had dealt with Death.
You had come to an agreement finally:
He could keep your Daddy and you could have a child.

Macabre debate. Yet it had cost you
Two years, three years, desperate days and weepings.
Finally you had stripped the death-dress off,
Burned it on Daddy's grave.
Did it so resolutely, made
Such successful magic of it, Life
Was attracted and swerved down –
Unlikely, like a wild dove, to land on your head.
Day of America's Independence
You set out. And I, not Death,
Drove the car.
                    Was Death, too, part of our luggage?
Unemployed for a while, fellow traveller?
Did he ride on the car top, on the bonnet?
Did he meet us now and again on the road,
Smiling in a café, at a gas station?
Stowaway in our ice-box?
Did he run in the wheel's shadow?

Or did he sulk in your papers, back in your bedroom,
Waiting for your habits
To come back and remember him? You had hidden him
From yourself and deceived even Life.
But your blossom had fruited and in England
It ripened. There your midwife,

The orchardist, was a miniature Indian lady
Black and archaic, half-Gond,
With her singing manner and her lucky charm voice,
A priestess of fruits.
Our Black Isis had stepped off the wall
Shaking her sistrum –
Polymorphus Daemon,
Magnae Deorum Matris – with the moon
Between her hip-bones and crowned with ears of corn.

The great goddess in person
Had put on your body, waxing full,
Using your strainings
Like a surgical glove, to create with,
Like a soft mask to triumph and be grotesque in
On the bed of birth.

It was not Death
Weeping in you then, when you lay among bloody cloths
Holding what had come out of you to cry.

It was not poetic death
Lifted you from the blood and set you
Straightaway lurching – exultant –
To the phone, to announce to the world
What Life had made of you,
Your whole body borrowed
By immortality and its promise,
Your arms filled
With what had never died, never known Death.

Epiphany

London. The grimy lilac softness
Of an April evening. Me
Walking over Chalk Farm Bridge
On my way to the tube station.
A new father – slightly light-headed
With the lack of sleep and the novelty.
Next, this young fellow coming towards me.

I glanced at him for the first time as I passed him
Because I noticed (I couldn't believe it)
What I'd been ignoring.

Not the bulge of a small animal
Buttoned into the top of his jacket
The way colliers used to wear their whippets –
But its actual face. Eyes reaching out
Trying to catch my eyes – so familiar!
The huge ears, the pinched, urchin expression –
The wild confronting stare, pushed through fear,
Between the jacket lapels.
                           'It's a fox-cub!'
I heard my own surprise as I stopped.
He stopped. 'Where did you get it? What
Are you going to do with it?'
                           A fox-cub
On the hump of Chalk Farm Bridge!

'You can have him for a pound.' 'But
Where did you find it? What will you do with it?'
'Oh, somebody'll buy him. Cheap enough

At a pound.' And a grin.

                           What I was thinking
Was – what would you think? How would we fit it
Into our crate of space? With the baby?
What would you make of its old smell
And its mannerless energy?
And as it grew up and began to enjoy itself
What would we do with an unpredictable,
Powerful, bounding fox?
The long-mouthed, flashing temperament?
That necessary nightly twenty miles
And that vast hunger for everything beyond us?
How would we cope with its cosmic derangements
Whenever we moved?

The little fox peered past me at other folks,
At this one and at that one, then at me.
Good luck was all it needed.
Already past the kittenish
But the eyes still small,
Round, orphaned-looking, woebegone
As if with weeping. Bereft
Of the blue milk, the toys of feather and fur,
The den life's happy dark. And the huge whisper
Of the constellations
Out of which Mother had always returned.
My thoughts felt like big, ignorant hounds
Circling and sniffing around him.

                              Then I walked on
As if out of my own life.
I let that fox-cub go. I tossed it back
Into the future
Of a fox-cub in London and I hurried

Straight on and dived as if escaping
Into the Underground. If I had paid,
If I had paid that pound and turned back
To you, with that armful of fox –

If I had grasped that whatever comes with a fox
Is what tests a marriage and proves it a marriage –
I would not have failed the test. Would you have failed it?
But I failed. Our marriage had failed.

The Gypsy

The Cathedral was there,
Impotent, for show, for others, for other
Ages. The spectacular up-spearing
Of its tonnage pierced us
With the shadow-gloom and weight of the sacred.
Not the first time I'd seen Rheims. The last.
I shall never go near it again.
The lightning stroke of what happened
Burnt up the silkiest, secretive, tentative
Map of France I was weaving
Ahead of us – as a spider weaves its walkway,
For our future, maybe. Our first
Exploration beyond Paris together,
Reconnoitring, note-making, enthralled
By everything. We sat in the square
Dunking our buttered croissants in hot chocolate.
You were writing postcards, concentrated.
In your mac. Midmorning, the air fresh.

The dark stub gypsy woman
Was suddenly there. Busy, business-like
As a weasel testing every crevice,
Or the blade of a waiter splitting oysters,
Flinging without a pause
The bad one into the bin, the top shell
Into the bin, then at the next, attentive,
Finding the key-hole. She was holding out
A religious pendant – a Nicholas, a Mary –
Palm upwards. Expert, without a side-glance,
Almost before she spoke you had refused her,
A practised reflex, sprung like a trap, hard

Your vehemence met her vehemence.
Her racing routine demand stopped at your 'Non.'
And she did stop, stung, stunned, as sudden
As if you had slapped her. Like a pistol her finger
Came up to your face, all her momentum
Icicled into a pointer: 'Vous
Crèverez bientôt.' Her dark face
A knot of oiled leather, a quipu,
Like Geronimo's. Bitter eyes
Of grappa-dreg revenge, old Gallic malice,
Raisins of bile. And as abruptly
She had gone on, hither, thither,
Among the tables and vanished, leaving her words
Heavier than the Cathedral,
Bigger, darker, founded far deeper –
My whole body taking their weight
Like a newer or much older religion
In me alone, to be carried
Everywhere with me – deeper catacombs,
And with a stronger God.
                              But you
Went on writing postcards. For days I rhymed
Talismans of power, in cynghanedd,
To neutralize her venom. I imagined
Returning to Rheims, how I would find her
And give her a coin – bribe her to call home
Her projectile. But you
Never mentioned it. Never recorded it
In your diary. And I hung in a hope
You hadn't even heard it. Deafened, maybe,
By closer explosions. Closed, maybe,
In a solider crypt.

A Dream

Your worst dream
Came true: that ring on the door-bell –
Not a simple chance in a billion
But a meteorite, straight down our chimney,
With our name on it.

Not dreams, I had said, but fixed stars
Govern a life. A thirst of the whole being,
Inexorable, like a sleeper drawing
Air into the lungs. You had to lift
The coffin lid an inch.
In your dream or mine? Strange letter box.
You took out the envelope. It was
A letter from your Daddy. 'I'm home.
Can I stay with you?' I said nothing.
For me, a request was a command.

Then came the Cathedral.
Chartres. Somehow we had got to Chartres.
Not the first time for you.
I remember little
But a Breton jug. You filled it
With everything we had. Every last franc.
You said it was for your mother.
You emptied our oxygen
Into that jug. Chartres
(I salvaged this)
Hung about your face, a mantilla,
Blackened, a tracery of char –
As after a firestorm. Nun-like
You nursed what was left of your Daddy.

Pouring our lives out of that jug
Into his morning coffee. Then you smashed it
Into shards, crude stars,
And gave them to your mother.

'And for you,' you said to me, 'permission
To remember this dream. And think about it.'

The Minotaur

The mahogany table-top you smashed
Had been the broad plank top
Of my mother's heirloom sideboard –
Mapped with the scars of my whole life.

That came under the hammer.
The high stool you swung that day
Demented by my being
Twenty minutes late for baby-minding.

'Marvellous!' I shouted, 'Go on,
Smash it into kindling.
That's the stuff you're keeping out of your poems!'
And later, considered and calmer,

'Get that shoulder under your stanzas
And we'll be away.' Deep in the cave of your ear
The goblin snapped his fingers.
So what had I given him?

The bloody end of the skein
That unravelled your marriage,
Left your children echoing
Like tunnels in a labyrinth,

Left your mother a dead-end,
Brought you to the horned, bellowing
Grave of your risen father –
And your own corpse in it.

The Pan

When he stopped at last in the long main street
Of the small town, after that hundred
And ninety miles, the five-o'clock, September,
Brassy, low, wet Westcountry sun
Above the street's far end, and when
He had extricated his stiffness
From the car crammed with books, carrier bags
Of crockery, cutlery and baby things,
And crossed the tilting street in that strange town
To buy a pan to heat milk and babyfood
The moment they arrived
Hours ahead of their furniture
Into their stripped new house, in their strange new life,
He did not notice that the ironmonger's
Where he bought the pan had been closed
And empty for two years. And returning
With the little pan he did not notice
A man on the pavement staring at him,
His arm round a young woman who wore
A next-to-nothing long evening dress
Slashed to the hip, and a white, silk, open-work shawl
Round her naked shoulders, and leopard-claw ear-rings,
He did not recognize, nor did his wife
As he squeezed back weary beside her
Behind the wheel of the Morris Traveller,
That this man, barely two yards from them,
Staring at them both so fixedly,
The man so infinitely more alive
Than either of them there in the happy car
Was himself – knowing their whole future
And helpless to warn them.

Error

I brought you to Devon. I brought you into my dreamland.
I sleepwalked you
Into my land of totems. Never-never land:
The orchard in the West.
                                    I wrestled
With the blankets, the caul and the cord,
And you stayed with me
Gallant and desperate and hopeful,
Listening for different gods, stripping off
Your American royalty, garment by garment –
Till you stepped out soul-naked and stricken
Into this cobbled, pictureless corridor
Aimed at a graveyard.
                                    What had happened
To the Italian sun?
Had it escaped our snatch
Like a butterfly off a nettle? The flashing trajectory,
The trans-continental dream-express
Of your adolescence – had it
Slammed to a dead-end, crushing halt, fatal,
In this red-soil tunnel? Was this why
We could not wake – our fingers tearing numbly
At the mesh of nettle-roots.
                                    What wrong fork
Had we taken? In a gloom orchard
Under drumming thatch, we lay listening
To our vicarage rotting like a coffin,
Foundering under its weeds. What did you make of it
When you sat at your elm table alone
Staring at the blank sheet of white paper,
Silent at your typewriter, listening

To the leaking thatch drip, the murmur of rain,
And staring at that sunken church, and the black
Slate roofs in the mist of rain, low tide,
Gleaming awash.
                    This was Lyonnesse.
Inaccessible clouds, submarine trees.
The labyrinth
Of brambly burrow lanes. Bundled women –
Stump-warts, you called them –
Sniffing at your strangeness in wet shops.
Their eyes followed you everywhere, loamy badgers,
Dug you out of your sleep and pawed at your dreams,
Jabbered hedge-bank judgements, a dark-age dialect,
Peered from every burrow-mouth.
                                        The world
Came to an end at bullocks
Huddled behind gates, knee-deep in quag,
Under the huddled, rainy hills. A bellow
Shaking the soaked oak-woods tested the limits.
And, beside the boots, the throbbing gutter –
A thin squandering of blood-water –
Searched for the river and the sea.

And this was what we had chosen finally.
Remembering it, I see it all in a bubble:
Strange people, in a closed brilliance,
Laughing and crying soundlessly,
Gazing out of the transparency
At a desolation. A rainy wedding picture
On a foreign grave, among lilies –
And just beneath it, unseen, the real bones
Still undergoing everything.

The Lodger

Potatoes were growing in the yard corner
That September. They were the welcome wagon!
First fruits of our own ground. And their flavour
Was the first legend. Pioneer
In our own life, those mornings –
I bought the spades, the forks, the overalls, the boots.
And the books. The books! I was a student
Gluttonous to swallow all horticulture,
The whole cornucopia. I began to dig.
I had to start right – I double-dug
The entire garden. And my heart,
And whatever hid in my heart, dug with me.
I assumed I was doomed – a matter of time
Before the heart jumped out of my body
Or simply collapsed. After a few hours digging
Suddenly something gave, the sweat burst out,
I was shaking. Heart. By now I was accustomed.
It could only be heart. The pangs. The poundings.
At night on my pillow the syncopated stagger
Of the pulse in my ear. Russian roulette:
Every heartbeat a fresh throw of the dice –
A click of Russian roulette. Strange
To be lying on my bed
Contemplating my heart as it knocked me to pieces,
As if I were attending the ache of a tooth.
And yet my heart was me. I was my heart.
My heart, that had always sung me through
My frenzies of exertion. How could it fail me?
I carried it everywhere with me, a dying child,
Weighing at my chest. A sudden spike
Under my left shoulder-blade.

Or a sword – horrible image of the thin blade
Pushed down vertically beside my neck
Inside the clavicle. Or a gnawing
At my ribs, from the inside. Worst
The unpredictable faintness – instant gear-slip
From infinite energy to ghostly nothing,
The drive jolted into neutral, and my motor
Racing uselessly. How many times a day?
Hypochondria walked, holding my arm
Like a nurse, her fingers over my pulse.
Well, I was going to die.
I started a diary – observations
Of my heart's errata.
My waking with strengthless hands. My going to bed
With fingers that throbbed so hard
They jerked the book I clung to and stared at.
The timing of the double-fisted blow
That came down between my shoulder-blades
'Soft but stunning like the kick of a camel'.
The sudden lapping at my throat of loose blood
Like a bird escaped, broken-winged,
From a cat briefly. Efforts to make my whole
Body a conduit of Beethoven,
To reconduct that music through my aorta
So he could run me clean and unconstrained
And release me. I could not reach the music.
All the music told me
Was that I was a reject, belonged no longer
In the intact, creating, resounding realm
Where music poured. I was already a discard,
My momentum merely the inertias
Of what I had been, while I disintegrated.
I was already posthumous.

[125]

Whatever I looked at, any cat or dog,
Saw me already dead, merely
Lurching on a few paces, perfunctory vision
Still on my retina.
                              My new study
Was all the ways a heart can kill its owner
And how mine had killed me. Of all this one,
Two, three years I told you nothing.
                                        Meanwhile
Who was using my heart,
Who positioned our bee-hive and planted,
With my unwitting hands, to amuse himself,
Nine bean rows? Who was this alien joker
Who had come to evict us,
Sharing my skin, just as he shared yours,
Watching my digging, so calmly? And gazing
Over your shoulder, into the poems you polished
As into this or that or the other mirror
That tried to ignore him?

Daffodils

Remember how we picked the daffodils?
Nobody else remembers, but I remember.
Your daughter came with her armfuls, eager and happy,
Helping the harvest. She has forgotten.
She cannot even remember you. And we sold them.
It sounds like sacrilege, but we sold them.
Were we so poor? Old Stoneman, the grocer,
Boss-eyed, his blood-pressure purpling to beetroot
(It was his last chance,
He would die in the same great freeze as you),
He persuaded us. Every Spring
He always bought them, sevenpence a dozen,
'A custom of the house'.

Besides, we still weren't sure we wanted to own
Anything. Mainly we were hungry
To convert everything to profit.
Still nomads – still strangers
To our whole possession. The daffodils
Were incidental gilding of the deeds,
Treasure trove. They simply came,
And they kept on coming.
As if not from the sod but falling from heaven.
Our lives were still a raid on our own good luck.
We knew we'd live for ever. We had not learned
What a fleeting glance of the everlasting
Daffodils are. Never identified
The nuptial flight of the rarest ephemera –
Our own days!
                    We thought they were a windfall.
Never guessed they were a last blessing.

So we sold them. We worked at selling them
As if employed on somebody else's
Flower-farm. You bent at it
In the rain of that April – your last April.
We bent there together, among the soft shrieks
Of their jostled stems, the wet shocks shaken
Of their girlish dance-frocks –
Fresh-opened dragonflies, wet and flimsy,
Opened too early.

We piled their frailty lights on a carpenter's bench,
Distributed leaves among the dozens –
Buckling blade-leaves, limber, groping for air, zinc-silvered –
Propped their raw butts in bucket water,
Their oval, meaty butts,
And sold them, sevenpence a bunch –

Wind-wounds, spasms from the dark earth,
With their odourless metals,
A flamy purification of the deep grave's stony cold
As if ice had a breath –

We sold them, to wither.
The crop thickened faster than we could thin it.
Finally, we were overwhelmed
And we lost our wedding-present scissors.

Every March since they have lifted again
Out of the same bulbs, the same
Baby-cries from the thaw,
Ballerinas too early for music, shiverers
In the draughty wings of the year.
On that same groundswell of memory, fluttering

They return to forget you stooping there
Behind the rainy curtains of a dark April,
Snipping their stems.

But somewhere your scissors remember. Wherever they are.
Here somewhere, blades wide open,
April by April
Sinking deeper
Through the sod – an anchor, a cross of rust.

The Afterbirth

Huddled on the floor, the afterbirth
Was already offal.
There was the lotus-eater's whole island
Dragged out by its roots, into the light,
And flopped onto blood-soaked newsprint – a tangled
Puddle of dawn reds and evening purples,
To be rubbished. You were laughing and weeping
Into the glare. A tear-splitting dazzle
Like the noon sun finally stared at
Had burst into the bedroom when the Gorgon
Arrived and ripped her face off
And threw it to the floor. Such a shocking
Beauty born. I saw it flash up
That sunburned German with all his strength
Slamming the sea-tripes of the octopus
Hard down onto our honeymoon quay –
In the blue-blackish glare
Of my sunstroke.
                        You were weeping
Your biggest, purest joy. The placenta
Already meaningless, asphyxiated.
Your eyes dazzling tears as I thought
No other brown eyes could, ever,
As you lifted the dazzler. I eased
The heavy, fallen Eden into a bowl
Of ovenproof glass. A bowl with a meaning
All to itself – a hare crouching
In its claret – the curled-up, chopped-up corpse
That weeks before I had jugged in it. I felt
Like somebody's shadow on a cave wall.
A figure with a dog's head

On a tomb wall in Egypt. You watched me
From your bed, through the window,
As I buried the bowlful of afterbirth
In a motherly hump of ancient Britain,
Under the elms. You would eat no more hare
Jugged in the wine of its own blood
Out of that bowl. The hare nesting in it
Had opened its eyes. As if some night,
Maybe with a thick snow falling softly,
It might come hobbling down from under the elms
Into our yard, crying: 'Mother! Mother!
They are going to eat me.'
                         Or bob up,
Dodging ahead, a witchy familiar, sent
To lock error beyond repair when it
Died silent, a black jolt,
Under my offside rear wheel
On the dawn A30. You heard nothing.
But it bled out of my pen. And re-formed
On my page. The hieroglyph of the hare.
You picked it up, curious.
And it screamed in your ear like a telephone –
The moon-eyed, ripped-up flower of it screamed.
Disembowelled, a stunned mask,
Unstoppably, like a burst artery,
The hare in the bowl screamed –

Setebos

Who could play Miranda?
Only you. Ferdinand – only me.
And it was like that, yes, it was like that.
I never questioned. Your mother
Played Prospero, flying her magic in
To stage the Masque, and bless the marriage,
Eavesdropping on the undervoices
Of the honeymooners in Paris
And smiling on the stair at her reflection
In the dark wall. My wreckage
Was all of a sudden a new wardrobe, unworn,
Even gold in my teeth. Ariel
Entertained us night and day.
The voices and sounds and sweet airs
Were our aura. Ariel was our aura.
Both of us alternated
Caliban our secret, who showed us
The sweetest, the freshest, the wildest
And loved us as we loved. Sycorax,
The rind of our garden's emptied quince,
Bobbed in the hazy surf at the horizon
Offshore, in the wings
Of the heavens, like a director
Studying the scenes to come.

Then the script overtook us. Caliban
Reverted to type. I heard
The bellow in your voice
That made my nape-hair prickle when you sang
How you were freed from the Elm. I lay
In the labyrinth of a cowslip

Without a clue. I heard the Minotaur
Coming down its tunnel-groove
Of old faults deep and bitter. King Minos,
Alias Otto – his bellow
Winding into murderous music. Which play
Were we in? Too late to find you
And get to my ship. The moon, off her moorings,
Tossed in tempest. Your bellowing song
Was a scream inside a bronze
Bull being roasted. The laughter
Of Sycorax was thunder and lightning
And black downpour. She hurled
Prospero's head at me,
A bounding thunderbolt, a jumping cracker.
The moon's horns
Plunged and tossed. I heard your cries
Bugling through the hot bronze:
'Who has dismembered us?' I crawled
Under a gabardine, hugging tight
All I could of me, hearing the cry
Now of hounds.

A Short Film

It was not meant to hurt.
It had been made for happy remembering
By people who were still too young
To have learned about memory.

Now it is a dangerous weapon, a time-bomb,
Which is a kind of body-bomb, long-term, too.
Only film, a few frames of you skipping, a few seconds,
You aged about ten there, skipping and still skipping.

Not very clear grey, made out of mist and smudge,
This thing has a fine fuse, less a fuse
Than a wavelength attuned, an electronic detonator
To what lies in your grave inside us.

And how that explosion would hurt
Is not just an idea of horror but a flash of fine sweat
Over the skin-surface, a bracing of nerves
For something that has already happened.

The Rag Rug

Somebody had made one. You admired it.
So you began to make your rag rug.
You needed to do it. Played on by lightnings
You needed an earth. Maybe. Or needed
To pull something out of yourself –
Some tapeworm of the psyche. I was simply
Happy to watch your scissors being fearless
As you sliced your old wool dresses,
Your cast-offs, once so costly,
Into bandages. Dark venous blood,
Daffodil yellow. You plaited them
Into a rope. You massaged them
Into the new life of a motley viper
That writhed out of the grave
Of your wardrobe. Like the buried wrapping
Of old mummy non-selves. You bowed
Like a potter
Over the turning hub of your rich rag rug
That widened its wheel,
Searching out the perimeter of a music –
The tongues of the loose ends flickering in air,
Issuing like a fugue out of the whorls
Of your fingertips. It calmed you,
Creating the serpent that coiled
Into a carpet. And the carpet
Lifted us, as it turned and returned,
Out of that crimson room of our cardiac days.
It freed me. It freed you
To do something that seemed almost nothing.
Whenever you worked at your carpet I felt happy.
Then I could read Conrad's novels to you.

I could cradle your freed mind in my voice,
Chapter by chapter, sentence by sentence,
Word by word: *The Heart of Darkness*,
The Secret Sharer. The same, I could feel
Your fingers caressing my reading, hour after hour,
Fitting together the serpent's jumbled rainbow.
I was like the snake-charmer – my voice
Swaying you over your heaped coils. While you
Unearthed something deeper than our verses.
A knowledge like the halves of a broken magnet.

I remember
Those long, crimson-shadowed evenings of ours
More like the breath-held camera moments
Of reaching to touch a falcon that does not fly off.
As if I held your hand to stroke a falcon
With your hand.
                          Later (not much later)
Your diary confided to whoever
What furies you bled into that rug.
As if you had dragged it, like your own entrails,
Out through your navel.

Was I the child or the mother? Did you braid it,
That umbilicus between us,
To free yourself from my contraction or was it
Pushing me out and away? Did you coil it,
Your emergency magic operation,
To draw off the tangle of numb distance
Secreting itself between us? Or was it
A drooled curse
From some old bitter woman's rusty mouth
That stays awake when she sleeps – her malediction

Spellbinding tiered labyrinths of confusion
Into the breadth of a hearth-rug? The coils,
Impassable, became a mamba, fatal.
Its gentle tap, when you trod on it for finality,
Would alter your blood. When I stepped over it
Would alter my nerves and brain.

                           I dreamed of our house
Before we ever found it. A great snake
Lifted its head from a well in the middle of the house
Exactly where the well is, beneath its slab,
In the middle of the house.
A golden serpent, thick as a child's body,
Eased from the opened well. And poured out
Through the back door, a length that seemed unending –
Till its tail tapered over the threshold,
The deep-worn, cracked threshold, soon to be ours.
That was after the whole house, in my dream,
Had capsized. And a perfect replica
Double of the house – the well-world's own
Upside-down reflection duplicate –
Had swung uppermost, and locked upright
Under its different stars, with an earthquake jolt,
Shaking the snake awake.

                         The rag rug
That had heaped out onto your lap
Slid to the floor. There it lay, coiled
Between us. However it came,
And wherever it found its tongue, its fang, its meaning,
It survived our Eden.

The Table

I wanted to make you a solid writing-table
That would last a lifetime.
I bought a broad elm plank two inches thick,
The wild bark surfing along one edge of it,
Rough-cut for coffin timber. Coffin elm
Finds a new life, with its corpse,
Drowned in the waters of earth. It gives the dead
Protection for a slightly longer voyage
Than beech or ash or pine might. With a plane
I revealed a perfect landing pad
For your inspiration. I did not
Know I had made and fitted a door
Opening downwards into your Daddy's grave.

You bent over it, euphoric
With your Nescafé every morning.
Like an animal, smelling the wild air,
Listening into its own ailment,
Then finding the exact herb.
It did not take you long
To divine in the elm, following your pen,
The words that would open it. Incredulous
I saw rise through it, in broad daylight,
Your Daddy resurrected,
Blue-eyed, that German cuckoo
Still calling the hour,
Impersonating your whole memory.
He limped up through it
Into our house. While I slept he snuggled
Shivering between us. Turning to touch me
You recognized him. 'Wait!' I said. 'Wait!

What's this?' My incomprehension
Deafened by his language – a German
Outside my wavelengths. I woke wildly
Into a deeper sleep. And I sleepwalked
Like an actor with his script
Blindfold through the looking glass. I embraced
Lady Death, your rival,
As if the role were written on my eyelids
In letters of phosphorus. With your arms locked
Round him, in joy, he took you
Down through the elm door.
He had got what he wanted.
I woke up on the empty stage with the props,
The paltry painted masks. And the script
Ripped up and scattered, its code scrambled,
Like the blades and slivers
Of a shattered mirror.

And now your peanut-crunchers can stare
At the ink-stains, the sigils
Where you engraved your letters to him
Cursing and imploring. No longer a desk.
No longer a door. Once more simply a board.
The roof of a coffin
Detached in the violence
From your upward gaze.
It bobbed back to the surface –
It washed up, far side of the Atlantic,
A curio,
Scoured of the sweat I soaked into
Finding your father for you and then
Leaving you to him.

Apprehensions

Your writing was also your fear,
At times it was your terror, that all
Your wedding presents, your dreams, your husband
Would be taken from you
By the terror's goblins. Your typewriter
Would be taken. Your sewing-machine. Your children.
All would be taken.
This fear was the colour of your desk-top,
You almost knew its features.
That grain was like its skin, you could stroke it.
You could taste it in your milky coffee.
It made a noise like your typewriter.
It hid in its own jujus –
Your mantelpiece mermaid of terracotta.
Your coppery fondue pan. Your linen. Your curtains.
You stared at these. You knew it was there.
It hid in your Schaeffer pen –

That was its favourite place. Whenever you wrote
You would stop, mid-word,
To look at it more closely, black, fat,
Between your fingers –
The swelling terror that would any moment
Suddenly burst out and take from you
Your husband, your children, your body, your life.
You could see it, there, in your pen.

Somebody took that too.

Dream Life

As if you descended in each night's sleep
Into your father's grave
You seemed afraid to look, or to remember next morning
What you had seen. When you did remember
Your dreams were of a sea clogged with corpses,
Death-camp atrocities, mass amputations.

Your sleep was a bloody shrine, it seemed.
And the sacred relic of it
Your father's gangrenous, cut-off leg.
No wonder you feared sleep.
No wonder you woke, saying: 'No dreams.'

What was the liturgy
Of that nightly service, that cult
Where you were the priestess?
Were those poems your salvaged fragments of it?

Your day-waking was a harrowed safety
You tried to cling to – not knowing
What had frightened you
Or where your poetry followed you from
With its blood-sticky feet. Each night
I hypnotized calm into you,
Courage, understanding and calm.
Did it help? Each night you descended again
Into the temple-crypt,
That private, primal cave
Under the public dome of father-worship.
All night you lolled unconscious
Over the crevasse

[141]

Inhaling the oracle
That spoke only conclusions.

Hackings-off of real limbs,
Smoke of the hospital incinerator,
Carnival beggars on stumps,
The gas-chamber and the oven
Of the camera's war – all this
Was the anatomy of your God of Sleep,
His blue eyes – the sleepless electrodes
In your temples

Preparing his Feast of Atonement.

Perfect Light

There you are, in all your innocence,
Sitting among your daffodils, as in a picture
Posed as for the title: 'Innocence'.
Perfect light in your face lights it up
Like a daffodil. Like any one of those daffodils
It was to be your only April on earth
Among your daffodils. In your arms,
Like a teddy bear, your new son,
Only a few weeks into his innocence.
Mother and infant, as in the Holy portrait.
And beside you, laughing up at you,
Your daughter, barely two. Like a daffodil
You turn your face down to her, saying something.
Your words were lost in the camera.

                         And the knowledge
Inside the hill on which you are sitting,
A moated fort hill, bigger than your house,
Failed to reach the picture. While your next moment,
Coming towards you like an infantryman
Returning slowly out of no-man's-land,
Bowed under something, never reached you –
Simply melted into the perfect light.

The Rabbit Catcher

It was May. How had it started? What
Had bared our edges? What quirky twist
Of the moon's blade had set us, so early in the day,
Bleeding each other? What had I done? I had
Somehow misunderstood. Inaccessible
In your dybbuk fury, babies
Hurled into the car, you drove. We surely
Had been intending a day's outing,
Somewhere on the coast, an exploration –
So you started driving.
                                        What I remember
Is thinking: She'll do something crazy. And I ripped
The door open and jumped in beside you.
So we drove West. West. Cornish lanes
I remember, a simmering truce
As you stared, with iron in your face,
Into some remote thunderscape
Of some unworldly war. I simply
Trod accompaniment, carried babies,
Waited for you to come back to nature.
We tried to find the coast. You
Raged against our English private greed
Of fencing off all coastal approaches,
Hiding the sea from roads, from all inland.
You despised England's grubby edges when you got there.
That day belonged to the furies. I searched the map
To penetrate the farms and private kingdoms.
Finally a gateway. It was a fresh day,
Full May. Somewhere I'd bought food.
We crossed a field and came to the open
Blue push of sea-wind. A gorse cliff,

Brambly, oak-packed combes. We found
An eyrie hollow, just under the cliff-top.
It seemed perfect to me. Feeding babies,
Your Germanic scowl, edged like a helmet,
Would not translate itself. I sat baffled.
I was a fly outside on the window-pane
Of my own domestic drama. You refused to lie there
Being indolent, you hated it.
That flat, draughty plate was not an ocean.
You had to be away and you went. And I
Trailed after like a dog, along the cliff-top field-edge,
Over a wind-matted oak-wood –
And I found a snare.
Copper-wire gleam, brown cord, human contrivance,
Sitting new-set. Without a word
You tore it up and threw it into the trees.

I was aghast. Faithful
To my country gods – I saw
The sanctity of a trapline desecrated.
You saw blunt fingers, blood in the cuticles,
Clamped round a blue mug. I saw
Country poverty raising a penny,
Filling a Sunday stewpot. You saw baby-eyed
Strangled innocents, I saw sacred
Ancient custom. You saw snare after snare
And went ahead, riving them from their roots
And flinging them down the wood. I saw you
Ripping up precarious, precious saplings
Of my heritage, hard-won concessions
From the hangings and the transportations
To live off the land. You cried: 'Murderers!'
You were weeping with a rage

That cared nothing for rabbits. You were locked
Into some chamber gasping for oxygen
Where I could not find you, or really hear you,
Let alone understand you.

                           In those snares
You'd caught something.
Had you caught something in me,
Nocturnal and unknown to me? Or was it
Your doomed self, your tortured, crying,
Suffocating self? Whichever,
Those terrible, hypersensitive
Fingers of your verse closed round it and
Felt it alive. The poems, like smoking entrails,
Came soft into your hands.

Suttee

In the myth of your first death our deity
Was yourself resurrected.
Yourself reborn. The holy one.
Day in day out that was our worship –
Tending the white birth-bed of your rebirth,
The unforthcoming delivery, the all-but-born,
The ought-by-now-to-be-born.

We were patient.
The gruelling prolongueur of your labour-pangs
Gave our dedication altitude.
What would you be – begotten
By that savage act of yours committed
On your body, battering your face to the concrete,
Leaving yourself for dead
(And hoping you were dead) for three days?

We feared
Our new birth might be damaged,
Injured in that death-struggle conception.
Our hope was also dread. The dolorous
Agony you performed was also happy:
The part of your own mother. I was midwife.
And the daily busyness of life
Was no more than more towels, kettles
Of hot water, then the rubber mask
Of anaesthetic that had no gas in it,
The placebo you kept grabbing for,
Gulping it like cocaine.

Your labour frightened you.
What was trying to come frightened you.
You had no idea what it might be –
Yet it was the only thing you wanted.
Night after night, weeks, months, years
I bowed there, as if over a page,
Coaxing it to happen,
Laying my ear to our unborn and its heartbeat,
Assuaging your fears. Massaging
Your cramps into sleep with hypnosis
And whispering to the star
That would soon fall into our straw –
Till suddenly the waters
Broke and I was dissolved.
Much as I protested and resisted
I was engulfed
In a flood, a dam-burst thunder
Of new myth.
In the warp of pouring glair,
Me bowled under it, I glimpsed
Your labour cries refracted, modulating –
Just as in a film – not to the cries
Of the newborn in her creams and perfumes,
Not to the wauling of joy,
But to the screams
Of the mourner
Just after death far-off in prehistory.
After death and outside our time.
The now of it
A scream stuck in a groove – unstoppable.
And you had been delivered of yourself
In flames. Our newborn
Was your own self in flames.

And the tongues of those flames were your tongues.
I had delivered an explosion
Of screams that were flames.
'What are these flames?' was all I managed to say,
Running with my midwife's hands
Not to wash them, only to extinguish
The screeching flames that fed on them and dripped from
  them.
I could not escape the torching gusher.
You were a child-bride
On a pyre.
Your flames fed on rage, on love
And on your cries for help.
Tears were a raw fuel.
And I was your husband
Performing the part of your father
In our new myth –
Both of us drenched in a petroleum
Of ancient American sunlight,
Both of us consumed
By the old child in the new birth –
Not the new babe of light but the old
Babe of dark flames and screams
That sucked the oxygen out of both of us.

The Bee God

When you wanted bees I never dreamed
It meant your Daddy had come up out of the well.

I scoured the old hive, you painted it,
White, with crimson hearts and flowers, and bluebirds.

So you became the Abbess
In the nunnery of the bees.

But when you put on your white regalia,
Your veil, your gloves, I never guessed a wedding.

That Maytime, in the orchard, that summer,
The hot, shivering chestnuts leaned towards us,

Their great gloved hands again making their offer
I never know how to accept.

But you bowed over your bees
As you bowed over your Daddy.

Your page a dark swarm
Clinging under the lit blossom.

You and your Daddy there in the heart of it,
Weighing your slender neck.

I saw I had given you something
That had carried you off in a cloud of gutturals –

The thunderhead of your new selves
Tending your golden mane.

You did not want me to go but your bees
Had their own ideas.

You wanted the honey, you wanted those big blossoms
Clotted like first milk, and the fruit like babies.

But the bees' orders were geometric –
Your Daddy's plans were Prussian.

When the first bee touched my hair
You were peering into the cave of thunder.

That outrider tangled, struggled, stung –
Marking the target.

And I was flung like a headshot jackrabbit
Through sunlit whizzing tracers

As bees planted their volts, their thudding electrodes,
In on their target.

Your face wanted to save me
From what had been decided.

You rushed to me, your dream-time veil off,
Your ghost-proof gloves off,

But as I stood there, where I thought I was safe,
Clawing out of my hair

Sticky, disembowelled bees,
A lone bee, like a blind arrow,

Soared over the housetop and down
And locked onto my brow, calling for helpers

Who came –
Fanatics for their God, the God of the Bees,

Deaf to your pleas as the fixed stars
At the bottom of the well.

Being Christlike

You did not want to be Christlike. Though your father
Was your God and there was no other, you did not
Want to be Christlike. Though you walked
In the love of your father. Though you stared
At the stranger your mother.
What had she to do with you
But tempt you from your father?
When her great hooded eyes lowered
Their moon so close
Promising the earth you saw
Your fate and you cried
Get thee behind me. You did not
Want to be Christlike. You wanted
To be with your father
In wherever he was. And your body
Barred your passage. And your family
Who were your flesh and blood
Burdened it. And a god
That was not your father
Was a false god. But you did not
Want to be Christlike.

The Beach

You lashed for release, like a migrant eel in November.
You needed the sea. I knew not much more
About Westcountry beaches than you did.
We are surrounded, I said, by magnificent beaches.
You'd seen the cliffs – a slashed and tilted gorge
Near Hartland, where we'd picked blackberries
That first somnambulist week of your ecstasy
With your brother. But now you needed a beach
Like your drug. Your undertow withdrawal
Blinded and choked you. It darkened a darkness darker.
England was so filthy! Only the sea
Could scour it. Your ocean salts would scour you.
You wanted to be washed, scoured, sunned.
That 'jewel in the head' – your flashing thunderclap miles
Of Nauset surf. The slew of horse-shoe crabs
And sand-dollars. You craved like oxygen
American earlier summers, yourself burnt dark –
Some prophecy mislaid, somehow. England
Was so poor! Was black paint cheaper? Why
Were English cars all black – to hide the filth?
Or to stay respectable, like bowlers
And umbrellas? Every vehicle a hearse.
The traffic procession a hushing leftover
Of Victoria's perpetual funeral Sunday –
The funeral of colour and light and life!
London a morgue of dinge – English dinge.
Our sole indigenous art-form – depressionist!
And why were everybody's
Garments so deliberately begrimed?
Grubby-looking, like a camouflage? 'Alas!

We have never recovered,' I said, 'from our fox-holes,
Our trenches, our fatigues and our bomb-shelters.'

But I remembered my shock of first sighting
The revolving edge of Manhattan
From the deck of the *Queen Elizabeth* –
That merry-go-round palette of American cars.
Everywhere the big flower of freedom!
The humming-bird of light at the retina!
Then the weird shameful pain of uncrumpling
From wartime hibernation, cramped, unshucking
My utility habit – deprivation
Worn with the stupid pride of a demob outfit,
A convalescence not quite back into the world.

Now I wanted to show you such a beach
Would set inside your head another jewel,
And lift you like the gentlest electric shock
Into an altogether other England –
An Avalon for which I had the wavelength,
Deep inside my head a little crystal.

For some reason I'd fixed on Woolacombe Sands.
I had seen that mile of surf in its haze
But only across the bay from Baggy headland
Where the peregrine went over and the shark under,
And the seal came in, and the sea-flash
Was gathered and crimped, tucked and crewelled
Into needlework by the cliff-top flora –
A brilliant original for Hilliard's miniatures.

Your crisis came late in the day. It was dusk when we got there
After a steamed-up hour of November downpour

[155]

And black cars sploshing through pot-hole puddles.
The rain had stopped. Three or four other cars
Waited for walkers – distant and wrapped in their dowds.
A car-park streetlamp made the whole scene hopeless.
The sea moved near, stunned after the rain,
Unperforming. Above it
The blue-black heap of the West collapsed slowly,
Comfortless as a cold iron stove
Standing among dead cinders
In some roofless ruin. You refused to get out.
You sat behind your mask, inaccessible –
Staring towards the ocean that had failed you.
I walked to the water's edge. A dull wave
Managed to lift and flop. Then a weak hiss
Rolled black oil-balls and pushed at obscure spewage.

So this was the reverse of dazzling Nauset.
The flip of a coin – the flip of an ocean fallen
Dream-face down. And here, at my feet, in the suds,
The other face, the real, staring upwards.

Dreamers

We didn't find her – she found us.
She sniffed us out. The Fate she carried
Sniffed us out
And assembled us, inert ingredients
For its experiment. The Fable she carried
Requisitioned you and me and her,
Puppets for its performance.

She fascinated you. Her eyes caressed you,
Melted a weeping glitter at you.
Her German the dark undercurrent
In her Kensington jeweller's elocution
Was your ancestral Black Forest whisper –
Edged with a greasy, death-camp, soot-softness.
When she suddenly rounded her eyeballs,
Popped them, strangled, she shocked you.
It was her mock surprise.
But you saw hanged women choke, dumb, through her,
And when she listened, watching you, through smoke,
Her black-ringed grey iris, slightly unnatural,
Was Black Forest wolf, a witch's daughter
Out of Grimm.

Warily you cultivated her,
Her Jewishness, her many-blooded beauty,
As if your dream of your dream-self stood there,
A glittering blackness, Europe's mystical jewel.
A creature from beyond the fringe of your desk-lamp.
Who was this Lilith of abortions
Touching the hair of your children
With tiger-painted nails?

Her speech Harrod's, Hitler's mutilations
Kept you company, weeding the onions.
An ex-Nazi Youth Sabra. Her father
Doctor to the Bolshoi Ballet.

She was helpless too.
None of us could wake up.
Nightmare looked out at the poppies.
She sat there, in her soot-wet mascara,
In flame-orange silks, in gold bracelets,
Slightly filthy with erotic mystery –
A German
Russian Israeli with the gaze of a demon
Between curtains of black Mongolian hair.

After a single night under our roof
She told her dream. A giant fish, a pike
Had a globed, golden eye, and in that eye
A throbbing human foetus –
You were astonished, maybe envious.

I refused to interpret. I saw
The dreamer in her
Had fallen in love with me and she did not know it.
That moment the dreamer in me
Fell in love with her, and I knew it.

Fairy Tale

Forty-nine was your magic number.
Forty-nine this.
Forty-nine that. Forty-eight
Doors in your high palace could be opened.
Once you were gone off every night
I had forty-eight chambers to choose from.
But the forty-ninth – you kept the key.
We would open that, some day, together.

You went off, a flare of hair and a plunge
Into the abyss.
Every night. Your Ogre lover
Who recuperated all day
Inside death, waited in the chasm
Under the tingling stars.
And I had forty-eight keys, doors, chambers,
To play with. Your Ogre
Was the sum, crammed in one voodoo carcase,
Of all your earlier lovers –
You never told even your secret journal
How many, who, where, when.
Only one glowed like a volcano
Off in the night.
But I never looked, I never saw
His effigy there, burning in your tears
Like a thing of tar.
Like a sleeping child's night-light,
It consoled your cosmos.
Meanwhile, that Ogre was more than enough,
As if you died each night to be with him,
As if you flew off into death.

So your nights. Your days
With your smile you listened to me
Recounting the surprises of one or other
Of the forty-eight chambers.
Your happiness made the bed soft.
A fairy tale? Yes.

Till the day you cried out in your sleep
(No, it was not me, as you thought.
It was you.) You cried out
Your love-sickness for that Ogre,
Your groaning appeal.

Icy-haired, I heard it echoing
Through all the corridors of our palace –
High there among eagles. Till I heard it
Beating on the forty-ninth door
Like my own heart on my own ribs.
A terrifying sound.
It beat on that door like my own heart
Trying to get out of my body.

The first next night – after your plunge
To find again those arms
Arching towards you out of death –
I found that door. My heart hurting my ribs
I unlocked the forty-ninth door
With a blade of grass. You never knew
What a skeleton key I had found
In a single blade of grass. And I entered.

The forty-ninth chamber convulsed
With the Ogre's roar

As he burst through the wall and plunged
Into his abyss. I glimpsed him
As I tripped
Over your corpse and fell with him
Into his abyss.

The Blackbird

You were the jailer of your murderer –
    Which imprisoned you.
And since I was your nurse and your protector
    Your sentence was mine too.

You played at feeling safe. As I fed you
    You ate and drank and swallowed
Sliding me sleepy looks, like a suckling babe,
    From under your eyelids.

You fed your prisoner's rage, in the dungeon,
    Through the keyhole –
Then, in a single, stung bound, came back up
    The coiled, unlit stairwell.

Giant poppy faces flamed and charred
    At the window. 'Look!'
You pointed and a blackbird was lugging
    A worm from its bottleneck.

The lawn lay like the pristine waiting page
    Of a prison report.
Who would write what upon it
    I never gave a thought.

A dumb creature, looping at the furnace door
    On its demon's prong,
Was a pen already writing
    Wrong is right, right wrong.

Totem

To ward it off (whatever it was) or attract it
You painted little hearts on everything.
You had no other logo.
This was your sacred object.
Sometimes you painted around it the wreath
Of an eight-year-old's flowers, green leaves, yellow petals.
Sometimes, off to the side, an eight-year-old's bluebird.
But mostly hearts. Or one red simple heart.

The frame of the big mirror you painted black –
Then, on the black, hearts.
And on your old black Singer sewing-machine –
Hearts.
The crimson on the black, like little lamps.

And on the cradle I made for a doll you painted,
Hearts.
And on the threshold, over which your son entered,
A heart –
Crimson on the black, like a blood-splash.

This heart was your talisman, your magic.
As Christians have their Cross you had your heart.
Constantine had his Cross – you, your heart.
Your Genie. Your Guardian Angel. Your Demon Slave.

But when you crept for safety
Into the bosom of your Guardian Angel
It was your Demon Slave. Like a possessive
Fish-mother, too eager to protect you,
She devoured you.

[163]

Now all that people find
Is your heart-coloured book – the empty mask
Of your Genie.
The mask
Of one that opening arms as if to enfold you
Devoured you.

The little hearts you painted on everything
Remained, like the track of your panic.
The splashes of a wound.

The spoor
Of the one that caught and devoured you.

Robbing Myself

I came over the snow – the packed snow
The ice-glaze hardened and polished,
Slithering the A30, two hundred miles,
The road unnatural and familiar,
A road back into myself
After the cosmic disaster –
The worst snow and freeze-up for fifteen years,
Twenty miles an hour, over fallen heaven.

I came to the house
In the blue December twilight.
Just light enough
To fork up my potatoes, to unbed them
From my careful clamp. I shelled off their snowed-over
    coverlet.
They seemed almost warm in their straw.
They exhaled the sweetness
Of the hopes I'd dug into them. It was a nest
Secret, living, the eggs of my coming year,
Like my own plump litter, my secret family,
Little earthen embryos, little fists
And frowning brows and the old, new sleep-smell of earth.

I picked over my apples,
My Victorias, my pig's noses,
In the dark outhouse, and my fat Bramleys.
My spring prayers still solid,
My summer intact in spite of everything.
I filled for you
A sack of potatoes and a sack of apples.

[165]

And I inspected my gladioli bulbs
In the dusty loft, in their dry rags, hibernating
(I did not know they were freezing to death).

Then I crept through the house. You never knew
How I listened to our absence,
A ghostly trespasser, or my strange gloating
In that inlaid corridor, in the snow-blue twilight,
So precise and tender, a dark sapphire.
The front room, our crimson chamber,
With our white-painted bookshelves, our patient books,
The rickety walnut desk I paid six pounds for,
The horse-hair Victorian chair I got for five shillings,
Waited only for us. It was so strange!
And the crimson cataract of our stair Wilton
Led up to caverns of twelfth-century silence
We had hardly disturbed, in our newness.
Listening there, at the bottom of the stair,
Under the snow-loaded house
Was like listening to the sleeping brain-life
Of an unborn baby.

The house made newly precious to me
By your last lonely weeks there, and your crying.
But sweet with cleanliness,
Tight as a plush-lined casket
In a safe
In the December dusk. And, shuttered by wintering boughs,
The stained church-windows glowed
As if the sun had sunk there, inside the church.

I listened, as I sealed it up from myself
(The twelve-hour ice-crawl ahead).

I peered awhile, as through the keyhole,
Into my darkened, hushed, safe casket
From which (I did not know)
I had already lost the treasure.

Blood and Innocence

In the wilderness
Between the locusts and the honey
They demanded it. Oh, no problem.
If that's all you want,
You said, and you gave it.
Your electrocution, with all its zigzags.
A St Anthony at the bad moment
The demons got him.
The flute-like soul sundered into all its needles –
Bamboo dynamited. Electrodes
Sizzling under your blond bang –
Your smile slightly tense. Waving their feelers
They tugged it away down their tunnels.

They came back. They demanded that other –
That one. Oh, no problem,
You said, easier in fact.
Yourself by Frankenstein, stiff-kneed,
Matricidal, mask in swollen plaster
Like Beethoven's. Magnified thumb
Under her Adam's apple, her tongue a foot long –
And herself a doll, your semblable,
Your pendant on a maple by Paradise Pond.
But yourself a babe again, born again
Not of mother's blood nor of Christ's –
Washed and reborn only in your own.

No, these weren't what they wanted. They wanted
That – that other. Oh, no problem,
Why on earth didn't you say.
Daddy unearthed. And the nine-year-old howl

Come of age
Round his good ankle, a cart-rope –
Hauling him into the light.
And a hoof-like thunder on the moor –
The gutturals of Thor
For accompaniment
To the howl.

Thor's voice its very self
Doing a hammer-dance on Daddy's body,
Avenging the twenty-year forsaken
Sobs of Germania –

Grinning squabbling overjoyed they
Dragged it into the thorns. How is that,
Is that OK? you asked.
You looked round for some acknowledgement
From the demanding mouths

In a gilded theatre suddenly empty
Of all but the faces
The faces faces faces faces

Of Mummy Daddy Mummy Daddy –
Daddy Daddy Daddy Daddy
Mummy Mummy

Costly Speech

Manhattan's full moon between skyscrapers
Forbade it.
The new moon, her whole family of phases,
Running the gleam of the rails
From rising to falling forbade it.

Even the beaver, way up in Alaska,
Treading water, to watch your son
Doing something strange in a glide of the Deshka,
Forbade it.
Yosemite's oldest root on earth, needle
By needle was adamant,
Onto your daughter's page, with signatures.
Every prairie-dog in Wyoming
Whether or not it ate the grapes you tossed
Forbade it.
Bubbles from Yellowstone's boiling paint-pots
Forbade it. They dubbed their prohibition
Sound-track onto your snapshot portrait fixtures.
Even the sluggish fish in Pontchartrain
Lobbed out right beside you where you swam
To forbid it. Night after night.
Nauset groaned in its sleep
And mumbled and mouthed, to forbid it –
Miles of shuddering lifted and fell back
A thunderclap veto.
And from a distant land your grandma's
Wedding photo hurried to forbid it.

Just as your own words
Irrevocably given to your brother,

Hostage guarantors,
And my own airier words, conscripted, reporting for duty,
Forbade it and forbade it.

They were simple guards and all were yawning,
Ignorant how your left hand wrote in a mirror
Opposite your right,
Half of you mortified, half of you smiling.

And ignorant of the spooky chemistry
Of opportunity, of boom and bust
In the optic nerve of editors.
Ignorant of the tumblers in the lock
Of US Copyright Law
Which your dead fingers so deftly unpicked.

The Inscription

Snow-cakes banked the streets. Frozen grey
Barricades of dirty sugar. Hard
Cold. Cold
His morning flat in bright sun,
Sooted in Soho. Brick light. New light.
Cargo-dumped empty lightness.
Packing-case emptiness, lightness. Ice-breaker
Her bows had butted through, the missing supplies
Warm in her hold. Cracked through the frozen sea
A rigid lightning of icy but open water
Where she moved closer. So here he was.
She had got what she wanted – to see
The islet or reef or rock he'd ended up on.
Her eyes went over the walls and into
Every corner, like a dog in a new home. Like a dog
That had seen a rat vanish, that smelt a rat.
There was his bed, yes. There was his phone.
But she had that number. Most of all
She wanted his assurance, weeping she begged
For assurance he had faith in her. Yes, yes. Tell me
We shall sit together this summer
Under the laburnum. Yes, he said, yes yes yes.
The laburnum draped deathly in the blue dusk.
The laburnum like a dressed corpse in full yellow.
The huge clock of the laburnum stuck at noon,
Striking noon noon noon –
What kind of faith did she mean? Yes, he had faith.
He had promised her everything she asked for,
And she had told him all she wanted
Was for him to get out of the country, to vanish.
I'll do whatever you want. But which do you want?

Go together next week North
Or for me to vanish off the earth?
She wept, pleading for reassurance – that he have
Faith in her, and he reeled when he should have grabbed:
'Do as you like with me. I'm your parcel.
I have only our address on me.
Open me or readdress me.' Then
She saw his Shakespeare. The red Oxford Shakespeare
That she had ripped to rags when happiness
Was invulnerable. Resurrected.
Wondering, with unbelieving fingers,
She opened it. She read the inscription. She closed it
Like the running animal that receives
The fatal bullet without a faltering check
In its stride, she started again
Begging for that reassurance and he gave it
Over and over and over and over he gave
What she did not want or did
Want and could no longer accept or open
Helpless-handed as she hid from him
The wound she had given herself, striking at him
Had given herself, that had emptied
From her hands the strength to hold him against
The shock of her words from nowhere, that had
Fatally gone through her and hit him.

Night-Ride on Ariel

Your moon was full of women.
Your moon-mother there, over your bed,
The Tyrolean moon, the guttural,
Mourning and remaking herself.
It was always Monday in her mind.
Prouty was there, tender and buoyant moon,
Whose wand of beams so dainty
Put the costly sparkle
Into Cinderella. Beutscher
Moon of dismemberment and resurrection
Who found enough parts on the floor of her shop
To fill your old skin and get you walking
Into Tuesday. Mary Ellen Chase,
Silver nimbus lit, egg eyes hooded,
The moon-owl who found you
Even in England, and plucked you out of my nest
And carried you back to college,
Dragging you all the way, your toes trailing
In the Atlantic.
                          Phases
Of your dismal-headed
Fairy godmother moon. Mother
Making you dance with her magnetic eye
On your Daddy's coffin
(There in the family film). Prouty
Wafting you to the ballroom of broken glass
On bleeding feet. Beutscher
Twanging the puppet strings
That waltzed you in air out of your mythical grave
To jig with your Daddy's bones on a kind of tightrope
Over the gap of your real grave.

Mary Ellen Moon of Massachusetts
Struck you with her chiming claw
And turned you into an hourglass of moonlight
With its menstrual wound
Of shadow sand. She propped you
On her lectern,
Lecture-timer.
                      White-faced bolts
Of electrocuting moonlight –
Masks of the full or over-full or empty
Moon that tipped your heart
Upside down and drained it. As you flew
They jammed all your wavelengths
With their criss-cross instructions,
Crackling and dragging their blacks
Over your failing flight,
Hauling your head this way and that way
As you clung to the sun – to the last
Shred of the exploded dawn
In your fist –

That Monday.

Telos

Too many Alphas. Too much Alpha. Sunstruck
With Alpha. Eye-sick,
Head-sick, sick sick sick O
Sick of Alpha. You kicked school it
Collapsed in Alphas. You shook
The lightning conductor between your teeth –
All the sky-signs registered Alpha.
You burrowed for a way back out of it all.
Down into a cellar. There in the dark
Your eyes tight shut
You turned your mother inside out
Like ripping a feather-pillow
And came up covered with Alphas.
You stamped and stamped
Like Rumpelstiltskin
On your Daddy's coffin and the whole band
Started up Alpha. The whole stadium
Clapped Alpha, roared Alpha. You sniped at
Ping-pong balls boy-friend after boy-friend
Jogging on pin-jet fountains and bull's-eyed
A straight row of Alphas. Won a huge
Plastic Alpha with blond hanks. You smashed her
With a kitchen stool and out fell
Tick-tock Alpha. Bloodprints
Of your escaping heel
Signed the street-scene snowscape Alpha.

                                        Anyhow,

Anywhere to lose
The Furies of Alpha you crawled under
Or hurdled every letter in the Alphabet

[176]

And hurling yourself beyond Omega
                                    fell
Into a glittering Universe of Alpha.

Brasilia

You returned
In your steel helm. Helpless
We were dragged into court, your arena,
Gagged in the hush.
Titterings of horror
And the bead of sweat in the spine's furrow.
You delivered
The three sentences. Not a whisper
In the hush.
Your great love had spoken.
Only the most horrible crime
Could have brought down
The blade of lightning
That descended then. Dazzled,
All coughed in the ozone.
Even the dogs were stunned. And the same flash
Snatched you up into Heaven.
Some Colosseum flunkeys
Carry out your father's body.
Another carries his head. Your mother
Stands, and to huge amazement
Staggers out, carrying her own head.
Other flunkeys carry me and mine.

Every day since, throughout your Empire,
Like the motherly wraith who nightly
Wailed through the streets of Tenochtitlán
Just before Cortés ended it –
Your effigies cry out on their plinths,
Dry-eyed. Your portraits, tearlessly,
Weep in the books.

The Cast

Daddy had come back to hear
All you had against him. He
Could not believe it. Where
Did you get those words if not
In the tails of his bees? For others
The honey. For him, Cupid's bow
Modified in Peenemünde
Via Brueghel. Helpless
As weightless, voiceless as lifeless,
He had to hear it all
Driven into him up to the feathers,
Had to stand the stake
Not through his heart, but upright
In the town square, him tied to it
Stark naked full of those arrows
In the bronze of immortal poesy.

So your cry of deliverance
Materialized in his
Sacrificed silence. Every arrow
Nailing him there a star
In your constellation. The giant
Chunk of jagged weapon –
His whole distorted statue
Like a shard of shrapnel
Eased out of your old wound. Rejected
By your body. Daddy
No longer to be borne. Your words
Like phagocytes, ridding you with a roar
Of the heavy pain.

[179]

Healed you vanished
From the monumental
Immortal form
Of your injury: your Daddy's
Body full of your arrows. Though it was
Your blood that dried on him.

The Ventriloquist

We caught each other by the body
    And fell in a heap.
Your doll in the dark bedroom woke
    With her scream a whip.

With your arms around my neck
    I ran through a thorny wood.
The doll screamed after us, to the world,
    Daddy was no good.

You sobbed against my chest.
    I waded the river's freeze.
The doll had put your Mummy on show –
    The Kraken of the seas.

As you lay on the bed
    I leaned to the locked door.
The doll sat on the roof and screamed
    I was with a whore.

The doll broke in that night
    Killed you and was gone
Screaming at the stars to look
    And see Justice done.

Life after Death

What can I tell you that you do not know
Of the life after death?

Your son's eyes, which had unsettled us
With your Slavic Asiatic
Epicanthic fold, but would become
So perfectly your eyes,
Became wet jewels,
The hardest substance of the purest pain
As I fed him in his high white chair.
Great hands of grief were wringing and wringing
His wet cloth of face. They wrung out his tears.
But his mouth betrayed you – it accepted
The spoon in my disembodied hand
That reached through from the life that had survived you.

Day by day his sister grew
Paler with the wound
She could not see or touch or feel, as I dressed it
Each day with her blue Breton jacket.

By night I lay awake in my body
The Hanged Man
My neck-nerve uprooted and the tendon
Which fastened the base of my skull
To my left shoulder
Torn from its shoulder-root and cramped into knots –
I fancied the pain could be explained
If I were hanging in the spirit
From a hook under my neck-muscle.

Dropped from life
We three made a deep silence
In our separate cots.

We were comforted by wolves.
Under that February moon and the moon of March
The Zoo had come close.
And in spite of the city
Wolves consoled us. Two or three times each night
For minutes on end
They sang. They had found where we lay.
And the dingos, and the Brazilian-maned wolves –
All lifted their voices together
With the grey Northern pack.

The wolves lifted us in their long voices.
They wound us and enmeshed us
In their wailing for you, their mourning for us,
They wove us into their voices. We lay in your death,
In the fallen snow, under falling snow,

As my body sank into the folk-tale
Where the wolves are singing in the forest
For two babes, who have turned, in their sleep,
Into orphans
Beside the corpse of their mother.

The Hands

Two immense hands
Dandled your infancy.
Later the same hands quietly
Positioned you in the crawl space
And fed you the pills,
Gloved so you would not recognize them.

When you woke in the hospital
You got help to recognize
The fingerprints inside what you had done.
You could not believe it. It was hard
For you to believe.
                          Later, inside your poems
Which they wore like gloves, the same hands
Left big fingerprints. The same
Inside your last-stand letters
Which they wore like gloves.
Inside those words you struck me with
That moved so much faster than your mouth
And that still ring in my ears.

Sometimes I think
Finally you yourself were two gloves
Worn by those two hands.
Sometimes I even think that I too
Was picked up, a numbness of gloves
Worn by those same hands,
Doing what they needed done, because
The fingerprints inside what I did
And inside your poems and your letters

And inside what you did
Are the same.

The fingerprints
Inside empty gloves, these, here,
From which the hands have vanished.

The Prism

The waters off beautiful Nauset
Were the ocean sun, the sea-poured crystal
Behind your efforts. They were your self's cradle.
What happened to it all that winter you went
Into your snowed-on grave, in the Pennines?
It goes with me, your seer's vision-stone.
Like a lucky stone, my unlucky stone.
I can look into it and still see
That salty globe of blue, its gull-sparkle,
Its path of surf-groomed sand
Roaming away north
Like the path of the Israelites
Under the hanging, arrested hollow of thunder
Into promise, and you walking it
Your sloped brown shoulders, your black swim-suit,
Towards that sea-lit sky.
                              Wherever you went
It was your periscope lens,
Between your earthenware earrings,
Behind your eye-brightness, so lucidly balanced,
Such a flawless crystal, so worshipped.

I still have it. I hold it –
'The waters off beautiful Nauset'.
Your intact childhood, your Paradise
With its pre-Adamite horse-shoe crab in the shallows
As a guarantee, God's own trademark.
I turn it, a prism, this way and that.
That way I see the filmy surf-wind flicker
Of your ecstasies, your visions in the crystal.

[186]

This way the irreparably-crushed lamp
In my crypt of dream, totally dark,
Under your gravestone.

The God

You were like a religious fanatic
Without a god – unable to pray.
You wanted to be a writer.
Wanted to write? What was it within you
Had to tell its tale?
The story that has to be told
Is the writer's God, who calls
Out of sleep, inaudibly: 'Write.'
Write what?

Your heart, mid-Sahara, raged
In its emptiness.
Your dreams were empty.
You bowed at your desk and you wept
Over the story that refused to exist,
As over a prayer
That could not be prayed
To a non-existent God. A dead God
With a terrible voice.
You were like those desert ascetics
Who fascinated you,
Parching in such a torturing
Vacuum of God
It sucked goblins out of their finger-ends,
Out of the soft motes of the sun-shaft,
Out of the blank rock face.
The gagged prayer of their sterility
Was a God.
So was your panic of emptiness – a God.

You offered him verses. First
Little phials of the emptiness
Into which your panic dropped its tears
That dried and left crystalline spectra.
Crusts of salt from your sleep.
Like the dewy sweat
On some desert stones, after dawn.
Oblations to an absence.
Little sacrifices. Soon

Your silent howl through the night
Had made itself a moon, a fiery idol
Of your God.
Your crying carried its moon
Like a woman a dead child. Like a woman
Nursing a dead child, bending to cool
Its lips with tear-drops on her fingertip,
So I nursed you, who nursed a moon
That was human but dead, withered, and
Burned you like a lump of phosphorus.

Till the child stirred. Its mouth-hole stirred.
Blood oozed at your nipple,
A drip-feed of blood. Our happy moment!

The little god flew up into the Elm Tree.
In your sleep, glassy-eyed,
You heard its instructions. When you woke
Your hands moved. You watched them in dismay
As they made a new sacrifice.
Two handfuls of blood, your own blood,
And in that blood gobbets of me,
Wrapped in a tissue of story that had somehow

Slipped from you. An embryo story.
You could not explain it or who
Ate at your hands.
The little god roared at night in the orchard,
His roar half a laugh.

You fed him by day, under your hair-tent,
Over your desk, in your secret
Spirit-house, you whispered,
You drummed on your thumb with your fingers,
Shook Winthrop shells for their sea-voices,
And gave me an effigy – a Salvia
Pressed in a Lutheran Bible.
You could not explain it. Sleep had opened.
Darkness poured from it, like perfume.
Your dreams had burst their coffin.
Blinded I struck a light

And woke upside down in your spirit-house
Moving limbs that were not my limbs,
And telling, in a voice not my voice,
A story of which I knew nothing,
Giddy
With the smoke of the fire you tended
Flames I had lit unwitting
That whitened in the oxygen jet
Of your incantatory whisper.

You fed the flames with the myrrh of your mother
The frankincense of your father
And your own amber and the tongues
Of fire told their tale. And suddenly
Everybody knew everything.

Your God snuffed up the fatty reek.
His roar was like a basement furnace
In your ears, thunder in the foundations.

Then you wrote in a fury, weeping,
Your joy a trance-dancer
In the smoke in the flames.
'God is speaking through me,' you told me.
'Don't say that,' I cried. 'Don't say that.
That is horribly unlucky!'
As I sat there with blistering eyes
Watching everything go up
In the flames of your sacrifice
That finally caught you too till you
Vanished, exploding
Into the flames
Of the story of your God
Who embraced you
And your Mummy and your Daddy –
Your Aztec, Black Forest
God of the euphemism Grief.

Freedom of Speech

At your sixtieth birthday, in the cake's glow,
Ariel sits on your knuckle.
You feed it grapes, a black one, then a green one,
From between your lips pursed like a kiss.
Why are you so solemn? Everybody laughs

As if grateful, the whole reunion –
Old friends and new friends,
Some famous authors, your court of brilliant minds,
And publishers and doctors and professors,
Their eyes creased in delighted laughter – even

The late poppies laugh, one loses a petal.
The candles tremble their tips
Trying to contain their joy. And your Mummy
Is laughing in her nursing home. Your children
Are laughing from opposite sides of the globe. Your Daddy

Laughs deep in his coffin. And the stars,
Surely the stars, too, shake with laughter.
And Ariel –
What about Ariel?
Ariel is happy to be here.

Only you and I do not smile.

A Picture of Otto

You stand there at the blackboard: Lutheran
Minister manqué. Your idea
Of Heaven and Earth and Hell radically
Modified by the honey-bee's commune.

A big shock for so much of your Prussian backbone
As can be conjured into poetry
To find yourself so tangled with me –
Rising from your coffin, a big shock

To meet me face to face in the dark adit
Where I have come looking for your daughter.
You had assumed this tunnel your family vault.
I never dreamed, however occult our guilt,

Your ghost inseparable from my shadow
As long as your daughter's words can stir a candle.
She could hardly tell us apart in the end.
Your portrait, here, could be my son's portrait.

I understand – you never could have released her.
I was a whole myth too late to replace you.
This underworld, my friend, is her heart's home.
Inseparable, here we must remain,

Everything forgiven and in common –
Not that I see her behind you, where I face you,
But like Owen, after his dark poem,
Under the battle, in the catacomb,

Sleeping with his German as if alone.

[193]

Fingers

Who will remember your fingers?
Their winged life? They flew
With the light in your look.
At the piano, stomping out hits from the forties,
They performed an incidental clowning
Routine of their own, deadpan puppets.
You were only concerned to get them to the keys.
But as you talked, as your eyes signalled
The strobes of your elation,
They flared, flicked balletic aerobatics.
I thought of birds in some tropical sexual
Play of display, leaping and somersaulting,
Doing strange things in the air, and dropping to the dust.
Those dancers of your excess!
With such deft, practical touches – so accurate.
Thinking their own thoughts caressed like lightning
The lipstick into your mouth corners.

Trim conductors of your expertise,
Cavorting at your typewriter,
Possessed by infant spirit, puckish,
Who, whatever they did, danced or mimed it
In a weightless largesse of espressivo.

I remember your fingers. And your daughter's
Fingers remember your fingers
In everything they do.
Her fingers obey and honour your fingers,
The Lares and Penates of our house.

The Dogs Are Eating Your Mother

That is not your mother but her body.
She leapt from our window
And fell there. Those are not dogs
That seem to be dogs
Pulling at her. Remember the lean hound
Running up the lane holding high
The dangling raw windpipe and lungs
Of a fox? Now see who
Will drop on all fours at the end of the street
And come romping towards your mother,
Pulling her remains, with their lips
Lifted like dog's lips
Into new positions. Protect her
And they will tear you down
As if you were more her.
They will find you every bit
As succulent as she is. Too late
To salvage what she was.
I buried her where she fell.
You played around the grave. We arranged
Sea-shells and big veined pebbles
Carried from Appledore
As if we were herself. But a kind
Of hyena came aching upwind.
They dug her out. Now they batten
On the cornucopia
Of her body. Even
Bite the face off her gravestone,
Gulp down the grave ornaments,
Swallow the very soil.
                              So leave her.

[195]

Let her be their spoils. Go wrap
Your head in the snowy rivers
Of the Brooks Range. Cover
Your eyes with the writhing airs
Off the Nullarbor Plains. Let them
Jerk their tail-stumps, bristle and vomit
Over their symposia.

       Think her better
Spread with holy care on a high grid
For vultures
To take back into the sun. Imagine
These bone-crushing mouths the mouths
That labour for the beetle
Who will roll her back into the sun.

Red

Red was your colour.
If not red, then white. But red
Was what you wrapped around you.
Blood-red. Was it blood?
Was it red-ochre, for warming the dead?
Haematite to make immortal
The precious heirloom bones, the family bones.

When you had your way finally
Our room was red. A judgement chamber.
Shut casket for gems. The carpet of blood
Patterned with darkenings, congealments.
The curtains – ruby corduroy blood,
Sheer blood-falls from ceiling to floor.
The cushions the same. The same
Raw carmine along the window-seat.
A throbbing cell. Aztec altar – temple.

Only the bookshelves escaped into whiteness.

And outside the window
Poppies thin and wrinkle-frail
As the skin on blood,
Salvias, that your father named you after,
Like blood lobbing from a gash,
And roses, the heart's last gouts,
Catastrophic, arterial, doomed.

Your velvet long full skirt, a swathe of blood,
A lavish burgundy.
Your lips a dipped, deep crimson.

You revelled in red.
I felt it raw – like the crisp gauze edges
Of a stiffening wound. I could touch
The open vein in it, the crusted gleam.

Everything you painted you painted white
Then splashed it with roses, defeated it,
Leaned over it, dripping roses,
Weeping roses, and more roses,
Then sometimes, among them, a little bluebird.

Blue was better for you. Blue was wings.
Kingfisher blue silks from San Francisco
Folded your pregnancy
In crucible caresses.
Blue was your kindly spirit – not a ghoul
But electrified, a guardian, thoughtful.

In the pit of red
You hid from the bone-clinic whiteness.

But the jewel you lost was blue.